Notes in the Lunchbox

Notes in the Lunchbox. . .

How To Help Your Child Succeed At School

By Barbara Reider

Sierra House Publishing • El Dorado Hills, California

Cover Design by Wende Heinen
Production by DesignWise
ISBN 0-9621156-1-4

Dedication

When I was a young mother, I needed a book just like this one. Instead, I stumbled along on intuition, luck, and Doctor Spock.

Fortunately, I had three wonderful little teachers who, as they grew, provided me with a continuous course in parent education.

This book is lovingly dedicated, therefore, to my three children — Susan, Chuck and David. Two of them are now parents learning from their own challenges, while "Uncle Dave" adds his support.

I hope that someday they lean back and smile with love and pride as I do, knowing that, no matter what, they did their best!

Acknowledgements

To my husband, Jim, who lovingly encouraged me to write this book and willingly transcribed my pencil scratches into print.

To all the great Brooks teachers, whose expert techniques with kids have helped me write this book.

To Kathy Reimer and Mary Ritter, who revised and advised; and to Wende Heinen, whose graphic talents enhanced the finished product.

To my First Grade Illustrators: Jessi, Mallory, Meggie, Steven, Jessica, Larissa, Kevin, Aubrey, Megan, Taryn, Ryan and Christine.

And to a bunch of wonderful friends who are the cheerleaders every writer needs!

NOTES IN THE LUNCHBOX
TABLE OF CONTENTS

INTRODUCTION

5 CHAPTER I The Significance of

Self-Esteem
Will My Child Succeed?
The Grapes of Anxiety
Determination of Parents
Toward Better Understanding
What is Self-Esteem?
Your Child's Self-Esteem Begins at Home

15 CHAPTER II   The Correlation With School Achievement

High Esteemers
A Teacher's First Glance
Setting the Scene
Words Have Power
Responses to Inappropriate Behavior

27 CHAPTER III Risk-Taking

Boosting Our Own Esteem
Modeling New Behaviors
Taking Risks and Making Changes
Risk and School Success
The Poker Chip Theory
See if you Recognize Yourself
Ideas to Encourage Risk-Taking

41 CHAPTER IV   Creating the Climate

Establishing a Caring Climate At School
Be a Kid Advocate!
Creating the Climate at Home
In the "Olden Days"
The Autocratic Approach to Parenting
The Permissive Approach
A Democratic Approach

55 CHAPTER V   The Components of Self-Esteem

A Sense of Connectedness
A Sense of Uniqueness
A Sense of Power

59 CHAPTER VI   A Sense of

Connectedness

The Need to Belong
Behavior Related to a High Sense of
Connectedness
Clues to a Low Sense of Connectedness
Reaction Behavior (1) Withdrawal
Reaction Behavior (2) Acting out
Building Connectedness at School
Classroom Techniques
The Origins of Connectedness
How Parents Build a Sense of Connectedness

77 CHAPTER VII   A Sense of Uniqueness

Behavior Related to a Sense of Uniqueness
Clues to a Low Sense of Uniqueness
Nobody Special: The Follower
Nobody Special: The Misbehaver
Building Uniqueness at School
Classroom Techniques
How Parents Build a Sense of Uniqueness

93 CHAPTER VIII   A Sense of Power

Behavior Related to a Sense of Power
Clues to a Low Sense of Power
Building a Sense of Power at School
Classroom Techniques
How Parents Build a Sense of Power

113 CHAPTER IX   Together We Make a Difference

Heavy Burdens on our Schools
Advocates for Education
Homework
Television
Building a Love for Reading
Tips From Teachers

Marta Jean carried a red lunchbox to First Grade with her peanut butter sandwich in it. Sometimes there was a banana and maybe a bag of corn chips. But whatever the edible contents, Marta Jeans's lunchbox always contained one intangible item more precious than 25 chocolate-chip cookies. That lunchbox contained LOVE, in the form of a little note:

> *Dear Marta Jean,*
> *Do your best in school.*
> *Tonight tell me all about your day.*
> *Love, Daddy*

I was Marta Jean's teacher. I watched her face beam as she sounded out each word, a child who knew without a doubt that she was loved. Did that daddy know he was building this little girl's self-esteem? Did he realize he was helping her succeed in school? You bet he did!

Many parents are aware of the significance of a child's self-esteem. What is not widely known is that self-esteem rates equally as high as I.Q. as a predictor of school success. Children with average intelligence and high self-esteem can be extremely successful in school., while those with very high I.Q. and low self-esteem can fail miserably.

Wise teachers have known for generations that it's not so much I.Q. as "I can!" They realize that it is those students who feel good about themselves and their abilities who are most likely to succeed. Conversely, those who see themselves and their abilities in a negative fashion usually fail to achieve good grades. Academic success or failure is more deeply rooted in concepts of the self than it is in measured mental ability.

Self-esteem, both high and low, begins at home. And

parents are the original teachers. When parents prepare children for school by building confidence in every way they can, they increase the likelihood of success. Their children will be willing to strive and persevere. To participate and cooperate with others. And to learn.

I see so many scared and discouraged kids begin to slip through the cracks toward failure. These are the kids who adopt defensive behaviors to cover their failure, behaviors such as blaming and fighting, or withdrawing and giving up. I watch them, as they approach teen years, drop out of school and turn to self-destructive solutions: sipping wine coolers first, then drinking beer, experimenting with drugs and hanging around in gangs. And I know that these children began dropping out of school in about the third grade. Not that they necessarily left the classroom!

Parents must learn to recognize the tell-tale behavior of low self-esteem when it is first exhibited by their children. It is only with this recognition that we can understand the feelings behind the behavior. We must stop and ask ourselves, "What are her inner feelings? What emotions stir his actions?" As we better understand what motivates behavior and misbehavior, so can we help children make better choices. And help ourselves become better parents.

There are many, many techniques to enhance self-esteem besides tucking a note in a lunchbox. This book provides dozens of ideas and techniques. This is a book written by a teacher for parents. From me to you. My goal is to help you help your child succeed.

Our children are now at the age of prevention. As we increase self-esteem so can we prevent problems, build confidence, foster responsibility, and promote success in later years.

Together we can make a difference!

The Significance of Self-Esteem

Dad pulls his car up in front of school on the first day of September. Beside him is his daughter, a bright-eyed first-grader. She unbuckles her seat belt and hops out with a kiss and "Bye Daddy." From the back seat her fourth-grade brother glances around for buddies, then grabs his lunch and heads for the school yard. The car door slams behind him. "See ya', Dad," he calls over his shoulder.

Nearby, several moms watch their five-to-twelve-year-olds in bright T-shirts and tennis shoes bounce off to begin a new school year. Elsewhere in the town, other moms stand in doorways waving at yellow buses that disappear around the corner toward school.

Will My Child Succeed?

It is an emotion-filled day. Parents gaze fondly after carefully combed blond hair, slim-fitting Levis or a new school jumper. But obvious fondness isn't the only emotion they feel. As their chests fill with love and pride, worrisome thoughts and feelings cause anxiety to show on their faces.

- "Will he do well this year?"
- "Can he handle fourth-grade math?"
- "Will she fit in and find new friends?"
- "Will she raise her hand and take part?"
- "Will he listen to directions?"
- "Will the kids choose him for the team?"

- "Will the teacher understand and cherish this precious child of mine?"
- "Will my child succeed?"

These are the same questions that ran through my mind as my own children lined up at classroom doors for first grade or sauntered off to the bus stop for junior high. I didn't know it then but my questions, like every mother's anxious questions, concerned my children's self-esteem. I didn't really mean, "Will she fit in?" But rather, "How will she feel if she doesn't?" I didn't mean, "Can he understand the math, write the outline, spell the words?" Instead I feared what would happen to his self-esteem if he couldn't.

Parents have good reasons to be concerned. Research tells us that although most kindergartners have high self-esteem (80 percent), the percentage drops to 20 percent by the fifth grade, while only 5 percent of high school graduates report positive self-esteem.

These figures warn us of dire outcomes, especially when we understand the full impact of self-esteem. Those of us who work with children are concerned, too. We realize that self-esteem is as important to personality development as good health is to physical well-being. We know there is a strong persistent link between one's self-esteem and school achievement. We know that self-esteem is essential to the development of leadership qualities, creativity and positive personal relationships.

THE GRAPES OF ANXIETY

No one has more opportunity to interact with anxious parents than elementary school teachers. As a mother of three for 33 years, and teacher of hundreds for 25 years, I've been on both sides of the desk — anxious parent and concerned teacher.

On one first day of school I remember approaching my daughter's third-grade teacher in her classroom. "You have Susie, my only daughter, in your class," I said, "and I want you to know I am a very apprehensive parent." Her teacher smiled sympathetically at me as I reluctantly walked around the corner of the school building to my own classroom, knowing first hand the trepidation felt by parents of my students.

During my years as a teacher, I have come to many conclusions about parents. I think of them as being hopeful and determined. They are usually conscientious, willing, and supportive. And almost always anxious! I know this because of questions I'm asked, like these:

■ Is my child getting along all right?

Which translates to: **Am I doing all right as a parent?**

■ Does he behave in class?

Am I doing all right as a parent?

■ Is she cooperative with other kids?

Am I doing all right as a parent?

Hear the anxiety? Being a parent is a never-ending, difficult task that causes us to frequently doubt our abilities. There is no magic wand bestowing knowledge and skill upon any of us. We desire high self-esteem for our children, along with happiness and confidence and love and success and inner peace. Yet nothing renders us less knowing than the daily responsibility of raising children. Often lacking confidence, we muddle along by reading parenting articles, asking questions, lamenting, listening, hoping, and often flying by the seat of our pants. And all the while, worrying!

But hooray for parents! It is this same disquiet that makes them wonderful, because the next step is a willingness to learn. Therein lie the grapes of anxiety!

DETERMINATION OF PARENTS

Parents I talk to are constantly seeking ways to improve. This book evolved out their search and determination. The very act of reading means you also share in that search because:

- ■ you know parenting is an awesome responsibility and isn't getting easier.
- ■ you suspect that raising children is the task for which we are least prepared as adults.
- ■ you feel a nagging uneasiness about teenage alcoholism, drug abuse and school drop-out rates.
- ■ you recognize that self-esteem is a factor in a child's success and you are determined to learn how to build it.

Hang on to that determination. According to the latest

PUT YOURSELF IN THEIR SHOES

Do you ever get down in the dumps? Sure, we all do. And we are people in charge of ourselves, reasonably bright and successful, who feel we're as good as the next guy.

Now try this. For a few seconds, close your eyes and recall a particular time when you felt down. Recall the physical sensations. Now get in touch with the feeling, perhaps in your chest or your stomach. Can you hold on to the feeling?

Tragically, many teenagers constantly feel that way. Those with low self-esteem often feel a dejection that ranges from discouragement to total despair.

research, low self-esteem lies at the core of most problems kids deal with today — problems such as drugs, alcohol, school failure, teenage pregnancy, youth suicide, truancy and dropout.

As I write this, the high school dropout rate is at an all-time high. Over 1.5 million teenagers are homeless, not all of them by choice. Every 78 seconds a teenager attempts suicide. Many succeed.

How could an unwed pregnant girl feel good about herself? How could a teenager contemplating suicide feel lovable and competent? To some young people today, the consequences of low self-esteem shape their lives.

TOWARD A BETTER UNDERSTANDING

In recent years the California Legislature pioneered an effort to address how social problems were linked to self-esteem. The StateTask Force to Promote Self-Esteem and Personal and Social Responsibility was established to promote well-being among all people. Researchers involved in the study focused on three main questions: 1) How is self-esteem nurtured and fostered? 2) How is self-esteem lost and destroyed? 3) How can it be restored?

To find information that could supply the answers to these questions researchers looked at:

- the family
- education and academic failure
- drug and alcohol abuse
- crime and violence
- poverty and chronic welfare dependency
- the workplace

The final report resulting from the California study is an unparalleled source of information.Now, other states in the nation continue to look to California for leadership as they form similar task forces. In our country and throughout the world, people are working toward a better understanding of self-esteem.

WHAT IS SELF-ESTEEM?

If we look in the mirror we might describe our physical selves by using adjectives such as tall, plump, pretty, ordinary-looking or brown-eyed. We might also describe inner qualities like shy, happy-go-lucky, strong-willed or lazy. By doing this we've drawn a word picture, a self with many facets. This picture is our self-concept of self-image.

Self-esteem is how we feel about this picture. Those feelings can be positive and happy, in which case we esteem ourselves highly. We feel reasonably proud, perhaps even special, lovable and competent. But if emotions about our self-image are negative, we might feel ashamed, sad, powerless and unloved. Doubting our own self-worth, we feel of no value to others. This is low self-esteem.

However, feelings of self-esteem continually change, evolve and unfold as we make new decisions and try to carry out new tasks. Self-esteem, then, is a personal assessment of worthiness made at a specific time. When we have a deep sense of self-esteem, we are glad to be ourselves.

A child's self-esteem, like our own, influences his or her creativity, integrity, stability and leadership abilities. It influences how aptitudes and abilities are used, what friends are chosen, and how the child relates to others. The importance of self-esteem cannot be overemphasized.

YOUR CHILD'S SELF-ESTEEM BEGINS AT HOME

In my previous book, *A Hooray Kind of Kid*, I addressed questions about the formation of self-esteem.

- Where does self-esteem come from?
- Within one family, how can there be such disparity of self-esteem among siblings?
- What roles do society and religion play in forming self-esteem?
- Does lack of family togetherness play a part?

A study conducted by a child psychologist, Dr. Stanley Coopersmith, indicates that the characteristic labeled self-esteem is not related to family wealth, education, geographical living area, social class, father's occupation, religious identification, having two parents in the home or whether mother works. [82] Coopersmith concluded that self-esteem stems from the quality of the relationships between the child and the significant persons in his or her life.

Who are these significant persons? You — Father and Mother! Coopersmith's findings show that both high and low self-esteem begins at home. Infants born with the potential for sound psychological health either flourish or fail in their environments, depending upon the parents.

Over time, children discover who they are from their parents. A young child looks to his mom or dad for the answers to these vital questions:

- Am I lovable?
- Am I capable?
- Are my opinions important?
- Am I worthy of respect?

When parents treat their children like worthy and important people, youngsters will grow up believing these things about themselves. Naturally, as they grow, the opinions of other people also become significant — people such as teachers, friends and siblings. However, children always watch for the reactions of their parents.

In truth, once solid self-esteem is established, the opinions of others are rarely able to immobilize a child. Moreover, this child who is raised to feel self-respect has the capacity to love and respect others. This child has the confidence to try, to risk failing and to persevere.

Since the principal goal of parenting is teaching children to parent themselves, independence is the road down which we point our children. Independence allows them to think for themselves and rely on personal decisions as they check their options. The result will be the confidence and self-esteem required to lead happy fulfilled lives.

In *What Do You Really Want For Your Children*, author Wayne Dyer writes, "While many may believe that talent, opportunity, I.Q., loving families, or positive outlooks are the real barometers for determining one's success potential, these are all secondary to the possession of a healthy self-portrait." [43]

Your child's self-esteem is a result of encouragement received from you on a daily basis. Both high and low self-esteem begins at home. And your child's success at school hinges upon that self-esteem.

2

The Correlation With School Achievement

A question I am frequently asked is, "How does self-esteem relate to school achievement?" Research tells us there is a direct, one-to-one relationship: as self-esteem and self-concept increase, so does school performance. Extensive data supports this conclusion.

For instance, in his book, *Self-Concept and School Achievement*, William Purkey reports, "Academic success or failure appears to be as deeply rooted in concepts of the self as it is in measured mental ability." [14] Robert Reasoner, author of *Building Self-Esteem. . . A Teacher's Guide*, agrees. "The presence of self-esteem clearly distinguishes the highly productive individual from the non-achiever and from those who drop out or turn to drugs or alcohol as a means of escape." [1] The authors of *How to Raise Children's Self-Esteem* plainly state that low self-esteem limits success in learning, human relationships, and all productive areas of life. [5]

HIGH ESTEEMERS

So much for research; now let's get down to our kids. To see how high self-esteem helps children in school, we must be aware that a successful student:

1) is open to new ideas
2) responds confidently to challenges
3) takes responsibility for assignments
4) checks for options and makes his or her own decisions

15

5) works toward self-structured goals
6) perseveres when first efforts fail
7) feels pride in accomplishments
8) views himself as capable
9) recognizes strengths and skills as well as weak-
nesses
10) willingly shares opinions, thoughts and ideas
11) feels liked by others
12) seems to have a bond with peers
13) is comfortable in most social relationships
14) feels secure

Educators say that students with these characteristics succeed in school. Therefore, classroom teachers strive to develop these characteristics.

A TEACHER'S FIRST GLANCE

Let's return to that first day of school described in Chapter 1. Outside the classroom kindergarten teachers peel five-year-old hands from the grip of their mothers, who walk away feeling a mixture of emotions. Second grade teachers pull closed their schoolroom doors with "Welcome Back" printed on them, after admitting a new group of 30 students. One by one, cars and buses drive away.

Inside the classroom, a teacher's year begins. Standing in front of her chalkboard, Mrs. K. watches as her new group slides into their desks. She wonders which ones will succeed this year and how hard she will have to struggle to keep the others from failing.

PUT YOURSELF IN HER SHOES

Will the real teacher please stand up? Imagine that you are a teacher, facing 30 members of the graduating class of the year 2000. You wonder, "Can everyone in this group read at grade level? How many know their math facts? Will my skills pull me through with the slow learners? Will my patience hold up with the rowdies? Is it too late to go into real estate?"

Teachers have moments like this. Each September they have to muster determination for the task ahead. They sometimes have doubts about their own value as well, forgetting momentarily how significant they are in the lives of children.

Hopefully, Mrs. K. once more will feel inspired and will reaffirm her reasons for entering the teaching profession. "It certainly wasn't for the money," she muses, "nor was it for national acclaim!" Then Mrs. K. smiles to herself as she recalls a statement made by author Robert Reasoner: "Our satisfaction lies not in money or status but in the quiet knowledge that we shape the future."

Mrs. K. is good at assessing her students as they walk in. Those with heads up, smiles on their faces, eager for new friends, ready to be liked and to like others, ready to learn new things, Mrs. K. calls "hooray kinds of kids." She has every reason to believe they will succeed, because these kids have confidence and high self-esteem.

Mrs. K. also observes others whose self-esteem appears shaky. Distinguished by their behavior, these chil-

dren fall into two distinct categories. First are the children who enter with faces averted shyly and shoulders hunched. They smile timidly at the teacher, hoping they'll be liked, hoping they can do the work, and hoping they won't be called on. There are also the show-offs with chip-on-the-shoulder attitudes, who push in front of others and constantly misbehave. "Cover-up kids" is Mrs. K's name for both of these groups because they are children who are covering their lack of self-esteem. Aware of the direct correlation between self-esteem and school achievement, Mrs. K. knows that these cover-up kids are headed for failure, either academic or social or both, and that to prevent it she is determined to do her best.

Another year begins.

SETTING THE SCENE

Randy, Paul and Brett are three of the boys in Mrs. K's second-grade classroom. They all live in the same general neighborhood and come from similar families. Although each boy is loved, they are being raised according to three different parenting styles.

When Randy leaves for school, he is sent off with negative remarks, criticism and ridicule. "That shirt looks terrible," Randy's mom comments as he heads for the door, "Can't you pick out clothes that match?" Randy escapes to the front porch, then realizes he's forgotten a book. "Might've known you'd forget something," his mother calls out as he leaves a second time. "Hurry up! And behave!"

Down the street, Paul is leaving too. But instead of criticizing, Paul's mother hovers. "Paulie, I'm afraid that shirt you chose won't be warm enough," she frets. "Let me run and get another one. Mother doesn't want you to catch another cold." As Paul slips out the front door he remembers a forgotten book. "I'll get it, dear," mother calls. "I should've reminded you about it." She fetches the book, then waves until he reaches the sidewalk, calling anxiously, "Be careful crossing that busy street!"

Meanwhile, Brett bounds for the front door as his mother watches him go. "Hey, Brett, you look good," she says, "That shirt and pants are a real original combination. I can see you're proud of your choice!" As Brett reaches the sidewalk he remembers his book. "Good thinking," says his mom. "See you after school!"

During class that morning Mrs. K. makes some announcements. "I need one volunteer to explain our new science unit to the principal when he comes in, and two more people to show him our experiments. Oh, yes," she adds, "I also need an announcer for the Reading skits, and someone to personally invite the other classes to join us. You may sign up for these jobs at my desk before recess."

What about our three boys? Do you think Randy or Paul will volunteer for these classroom jobs? Will Brett volunteer? Mrs. K. always notices which of her students regularly participate — the ones who accept challenges — and she recognizes confidence and identifies low self-esteem. Mrs. K. will not be surprised at the names that appear on her sign-up sheet.

As we watched Randy, Paul and Brett as they left for school, we began to see a relationship between their treatment at home and their self-esteem, which in turn will effect classroom participation. The way parents interact with their children creates an emotional climate in the homes. This climate can hurt or heal, humor or humiliate, build self-esteem or threaten its very existence. The negative climate in Randy's home harmed his spirit just as surely as the overprotective fearful climate created by Paul's mother.

Now assume that these boys' mothers continue sending their sons hurtful messages. Over the years Randy hears repeatedly, "This kid is such a pest. . . thank goodness summer vacation is almost over!" Meanwhile, Paul is told, "Don't climb that tree! Don't monkey with those

PUT YOURSELF IN THEIR SHOES

Imagine that you are a seven-year-old named Randy. When your mom says, "Can't you understand a thing? You're so stupid!" you conclude that this must be true — to a young child, parents are infallible. So you label yourself "stupid."

How do you feel?

Or imagine that you are Paul, whose mom issues constant warnings, "Don't use that saw. You'll hurt yourself. You're too little." The result, since she's an adult and must be right, is to label yourself "incapable."

What emotions do you feel?

tools!" No wonder Paul and Randy have low self-esteem! Dorothy Briggs in *Your Child's Self-Esteem* reminds us that parents understandably do lose their tempers, but the child who is ". . . immersed in verbal character defamation concludes, 'I guess I'm a pretty lousy person. If your own parents don't like you, who could?'" [14]

WORDS HAVE POWER

Throughout our lives we receive 140,000 putdowns, according to Dr. David Thornburg. Much of this criticism enters the subconscious, especially the criticism made by parents when we were little. Negative messages enter children's minds loudly and clearly: "I'm not worthwhile. She doesn't want me around. I'll never be much good."

In adulthood the mind remembers: "They said I'd never amount to much. No use trying. I always muff it, even my mother told me that." No question about it, words have power and parents are often guilty of abusing that power.

A recent study regarding parent-child interaction done in a midwestern university measured parent comments directed at two and three-year olds. Over a period of two weeks, researchers recorded 432 negative comments compared to 32 positive comments. That's a 14 to 1 ratio. A similar West Coast study revealed an even more devastating 25 to 1 ratio. What dreadful words must make up the labels worn around the necks of tiny children! By the time they are 4 years old, how would we describe their self-esteem?

As children go to their workplace, the classroom, they need the high self-esteem derived from positive comments made by their parents. Brett, the last in our trio of boys, was sent to school with powerfully positive messages. Through his mother's words we knew his shirt and pants didn't match, but her comments about originality boosted his pride anyway. And she wisely encouraged Brett's sense of responsibility for his book by taking none of it herself. Brett entered his classroom with the confidence needed to succeed.

Self-esteem-building words are spoken with respect. They encourage and show caring. They are words that make us feel good.

- ■ "I'm glad you're here."
- ■ "I can always trust you."
- ■ "Thank goodness you were a girl!"
- ■ "You're so much fun to be with!"

RESPONSES TO INAPPROPRIATE BEHAVIOR

When a child misbehaves a parent must convey negative information. But even then there are positive ways of dealing with negative behavior so that children can learn from the exchange. Once again, because children incorporate labels into their self-images, we must avoid letting them label themselves in terms of the harsh words spoken in reproach.

PUT YOURSELF IN HER SHOES

Imagine yourself a child to whom the following remarks are made. Which ones make you feel inadequate? Which ones tell you how your parent feels without inflicting blame?

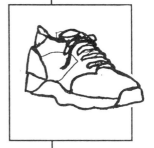

"You're lazy!" or "I'm worried about your grades."
"You're sloppy!" or "I get angry when you don't hang up your clothes."
"You're undependable!" or "I'm furious that you left my tools outside."

Notice that each phrase on the left begins with "You," while the less judgmental comments begin with "I." "I-reactions" are an effective way of dealing with inappropriate behavior because they address the behavior instead of the person. While it's not easy remembering to give "I-reactions," the results are worth the effort. Ultimately, this method motivates the child to be good, and there is no need for defensiveness since it tells the child, " Mom cares about me."

Parents do care. Parents are pedaling as fast as they can, and often on an uphill track. But the rewards for these parents are children who face each school day with confidence!

3

Risk-Taking

Are you aware of your own best qualities? Do you value your special strengths, your capacities and sensitivities? Do your actions show that you respect yourself? Or do you put yourself down? Do you practice assertiveness or do you allow others to run over you? Do you take risks or do you resist change?

BOOSTING OUR OWN ESTEEM

We can't afford to ignore our attitudes toward ourselves. "You do unto others what you do unto yourself," said psychologist Frederick Perls. If we can accept ourselves, we can accept others. If we do not respect ourselves, we seldom respect others. And we cannot give what we do not have. As parents we must learn how to raise our own self-esteem along with that of our children. Our goals for ourselves are the same ones that we hold for our children:

- to be enthusiastic about life
- to be happy individuals
- to be self-directed
- to take pride in our accomplishments
- to value ourselves
- to be creative
- to be risk-takers
- to be assets to society

Someone once quipped, "ninety-eight percent of adult Americans came from dysfunctional families, and the other two percent attended dysfunctional schools." Whether or not his statistics were correct, his suggestions were very relevant: this is a new day; let's work through the old stuff, then let it go and create new lives for ourselves and our children.

Most parents want to let go of dysfunctional patterns which were set in place as they grew up. Many of us try to raise our children in the way we would like to have been raised, and prevent our children from being hindered in their adult lives by what hindered us. Many of us have struggled with:

- lack of self-confidence
- lack of assertiveness
- low self-esteem
- fear of taking risks
- self-destructive behaviors
- conformity

MODELING NEW BEHAVIORS

We can look back at the examples set by our parents. Upon identifying the parenting methods and strategies which were helpful and those which were harmful, we can then make our choices as to which we will perpetuate in our own families.

For example, we know that assertiveness aids communication and builds self-respect. Yet many of us find that practicing assertiveness as well as promoting it in our children can be difficult. In her book, Dorothy Briggs describes a conversation between a young mother and her neighbor:

Mom: "If that son of mine doesn't start asserting himself, I'm going to explode!

Neighbor: "Give him time, he's only four. But what about you? You let people walk all over you.

Mom: "That's just the point. I can't stand it in myself, and I hate to see it in him!" [55]

If we want to teach assertiveness to our children, we must become more assertive. It is imperative to make our feelings and wishes known in a calm, assertive manner. Many times "I" messages are very effective. You might say:

- "I am irritated when. . ."
- "I feel hurt when. . ."
- "I consider it unfair that. . ."

These can be followed with assertive requests for changes, such as, "I want you to. . ., and "I'd appreciate it if you would. . ."

Teaching a behavior like assertiveness by practicing it ourselves is a technique called "modeling," which is especially helpful to teach values. If we want to teach our children to respect others, we ourselves act respectfully. If we want to teach our children to speak of their accomplishments and good qualities with pride, we praise ourselves. "Oh, no," you say, "That's bragging!" I used to believe that too, but I've since changed my mind. I now say to my class, "My handwriting is improving," or "I'm pretty good at singing." I model how to verbalize self-validations by my own example. It works! I now hear my students saying, "I'm getting better at drawing," or "I'm good at subtraction." They have learned to praise themselves.

TAKING RISKS AND MAKING CHANGES

Risk-taking is one of the most critical behaviors to be modeled by adults. Taking risks is what each of us must do to succeed, gain confidence, and build our own self-esteem. In fact, it is a key ingredient to self-esteem building.

We risk every time we make a change in our lives. When we suggest a new method of doing things at work, invite someone on a date or go on a diet, we risk failure, rejection and embarrassment. No wonder people resist changes. It's safer to stay and decorate the familiar walls of the ruts we put ourselves in!

Words borrowed from an unknown author remind us of the importance of taking risks:

"To weep is to risk appearing sentimental.
To love is to risk not being loved in return.
To try is to risk failure.
To live is to risk dying.
But the risks must be taken, because the
greatest hazard in life is to risk nothing. The
person who risks nothing gains nothing, has
nothing and can give nothing. Most
significantly, the person who will not risk
misses the opportunity to grow."

To build our own self-esteem, we must associate with people who are risk-takers and who treat themselves with respect. We should avoid those who are into self-put-downs, or who don't stand up for what they believe and want, and look for those who appreciate their own valuable qualities. Building our own self-esteem pays off, not only for ourselves but for future generations, as our children pass on their attitudes to their own children.

RISK AND SCHOOL SUCCESS

Kids also must risk in order to build confidence and self-esteem. Every one of these school situations requires a child to take a risk:

- raising one's hand to participate
- demonstrating an experiment
- reading out loud
- writing a composition
- stepping up to the board to write an answer
- stepping up to home plate to bat the ball

PUT YOURSELF IN HER SHOES

Imagine you are a third grade girl. It's 10:00 a.m., math time — not your favorite subject! As a teacher explains multiplication with zeros, she asks for three student volunteers to go up to the board. "Should I volunteer?" you wonder. I know how to do the problem, but what if my sweater looks dumb or my socks don't match?"

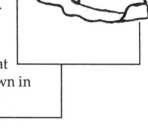

Your worries keep you from volunteering — the risk is too great — and so you slide unhappily down in your seat.

Seemingly inconsequential worries are big concerns to a child. In each of the situations just described, a child risks failure, put-downs, rejection by peers, or disapproval by the teacher. At a profound level a child risks personal self-esteem.

In the previous chapter a teacher named Mrs. K. asked her students to risk. The assignments for which the students were to volunteer required their verbal participation or demonstration in front of the group. We all knew which of our three boys was most able to risk, and we recognized his high self-esteem. We were aware of the emotional climate in Brett's home and the resulting relationship between his self-esteem and his willingness to risk.

THE POKER CHIP THEORY

Imagine that learning is a game of poker and that each student's self-esteem is a stack of poker chips. In any classroom we find a big difference in the number of chips students possess.

Some children might have 100 chips in their piles. How do they happen to have so many? Because of many past successes, both academic and social. Because of parent support and encouragement. And because the quality of relationships between these children and significant persons in their lives is positive.

When faced with a risk, these students push their chips right out on the table and say, "I'll try it. I'll explain the science project to the principal." As many successes increase their pile of chips they gain confidence and feel they can afford to lose a few. "Oh well," they say, shrugging off failure when they make a mistake, "I'll just try harder next time."

Other youngsters, however, come to school with only 15 chips of self-esteem in their piles. Why so few? Because of their history of recent failure, neglect, or lack of parental support. And because the relationships between these children and significant persons are negative.

Facing the same risks, assignments and challenges as high self-esteemers, these 15-chip kids are reluctant to gamble, reluctant to try. They dread failure and further loss. With so few chips, how could we expect such a child to risk willingly?

In fact, risking is so difficult for some kids that they quickly adopt the axiom: "If I don't risk, I can't lose." And so they choose one of two methods to cover up their feelings and their lack of self-esteem. We met these "cover-up kids" in chapter two as they trooped into Mrs. K's classroom on the first day of school. Some children — shy cover-up kids — slipped in meekly, hoping not to be noticed, while others — aggressive cover-up kids — elbowed in with chip-on-the-shoulder attitudes.

In general, shy cover-up kids:

■ avoid taking risks

- avoid any kind of attention
- withdraw or pull into a shell
- quit trying
- say, "This work is too hard. I can't do it."
  Translated to, "I'm afraid to try."

In general, aggressive cover-up kids:

- avoid taking risks
- cover lack of confidence with misbehavior
- act out for attention
- are undaunted by reprimands
- say, "This work is stupid. I won't do it!" Translated to, "I'm afraid to try."

Cover-up kids, lacking confidence, fail to experience the success gained by risking. School failure results, which further lowers confidence. Some call it a negative merry-go-round. As parents, we must teach our children to risk. But first it is important to understand how as parents, we actually discourage risk-taking.

SEE IF YOU RECOGNIZE YOURSELF

☑ Perhaps you are overly cautious. Do you issue continuous reminders about the dangers of life? "Don't climb that tree! Stay away from the edge! You're not old enough to go in the water!"

☑ Do you encourage babies to believe they are totally helpless by not allowing them to have minor struggles early? Do you rescue them when they crawl into an obstacle or pick them up when they experience a minor frustration?

☑ Do you allow your school-age child to conform to current fads because everyone else is doing it?

☑ Do you act as the referee in disputes between your children?

☑ Do you consistently schedule your children's activities for them?

☑ Do you remind your children of their limitations by saying to others, "He's not athletic. She can't carry a tune."

☑ Do you insist that your children ask permission for everything they do?

If these attitude and behaviors are similar to your own, think about the reasons you may be conducting yourself in this manner. While you don't deliberately set out to discourage risk-taking, you do receive a payoff for continuing the behavior. Is your payoff:

PUT YOURSELF IN HIS SHOES

You are a seven-year-old named Jimmy, reaching for independence, wishing you could be like the big guys. On Saturday you get out your bike and announce a plan.

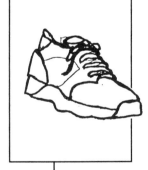

Jimmy: "Dad, I'm going over to Kenny's to build a treehouse."

Dad: "Just a minute there, son. Did you ask your mother? And you know you're too young for tree-climbing. You could fall and break your neck!"

Jimmy: "Dad, I promise I'll be careful."

Dad: "No. I'd rather you play here in our yard. Besides, I've already put out your croquet set."

- An easier job of parenting?
- A feeling of importance?
- A desire for power?
- Avoidance of failure as a parent?

In how many ways is Jimmy's dad discouraging him? By not accepting his grown-up way of announcing his plan. By being overly cautious, by criticizing Jimmy's ability, by scheduling his play time. What's the payoff for Dad? Dad's desire to be in charge reveals a power problem. If he were not into proving his superiority, he might have responded this way instead:

"Great idea, son. Thanks for letting me know where you'll be. Just play it safe on those high branches, okay? And how about if I come over later and lend you guys a hand?"

Transforming a home environment into a place where children can risk takes time and care. In addition, it often takes a change of attitude and a willingness to relinquish the payoffs. When parents see how self-defeating these attitudes are, they begin to consider new behaviors.

IDEAS TO ENCOURAGE RISK-TAKING

- Using wisdom and caution, encourage kids to explore and take chances like riding a unicycle, learning to dive, playing hide-and-seek after dark.

- Teach children to avoid being a slave to a fad. Talk about the importance of choosing clothes based on personal taste rather than what everyone else is wearing.

- Applaud children's dreams and goals, regardless of how improbable they sound. Rather than, "Don't be ridiculous," say, "Go for it!"

- Let up on pressure to win. Trophies are nice but participating is far more valuable in the long run. High grades aren't as important as knowledge. Too much pressure prevents risking a try.

■ Tell beginning preschoolers that, in their new school, they will be asked to try many new things. Give examples. Help them to know that it is okay to fail.

■ Let kids make decisions. Let them attempt extremely difficult feats. Let them try and let them fail. See them through it all.

"I DON'T KNOW HOW, BUT I'LL TRY"

On any given school day there are questions your child needs to ask, chances to volunteer for a team, or an opportunity to help paint a mural. Also, on any given day the teacher asks for definitions, requests the spelling of a word, or looks for someone to demonstrate shooting a basketball.

Time to volunteer. Some hands shoot up; some are raised tentatively, and some hands never go up.

Imagine a classroom where every student feels enough confidence to volunteer, where every chest swells with self-assurance, and where every child declares with determination, "I don't know how but I'll try." In my classroom this is the motto printed boldly up over the clock. As a teacher, I'm working on encouraging kids to risk, and as a parent you can too!

4

Creating The Climate

I hope you are a parent who creates frequent opportunities to visit your child's classroom. Perhaps you are a classroom helper; perhaps you have volunteered for some special event or have spoken to the class about your career. Hopefully, you make it a point to be there frequently, showing your interest.

Upon entering a classroom, I immediately become aware of the atmosphere, do you? There seems to be a wide diversity in classroom climate within any given school. Sometimes as I walk in I am instinctively aware of a special warm ambiance reflected in the faces of the students. I realize that here is an environment which is inviting, involving, and caring, and where no put-downs are allowed.

The classroom atmosphere that I have just described is an absolute prerequisite to risking! None of the ideas, activities or techniques designed in school to help a child risk would be effective without it, because a caring environment is a safe environment. Safe to try. Safe to fail. Children need to feel secure before they can risk the possibility of failure.

There are also certain houses where, as you immediately walk in, you feel "at home." You sense an accepting atmosphere, you know the family members care about each other, you recognize a team approach where each player knows that he or she is a contributing member of the team. Members are supported in finding their independence because each is unique in his or her own way. Kids are listened to and heard; cooperation is the modus operandi. A loving atmosphere prevails.

In this chapter we will explore the many ways that both teachers and parents create an environment supportive to school success.

ESTABLISHING A CARING CLIMATE AT SCHOOL

A skillful teacher can create a warm classroom climate. Haim Ginott, author of *Teacher and Child*, must have known the significance of that statement, for he wrote these words at the beginning of his teaching career:

"I have come to a frightening conclusion. I am the decisive element in the classroom. It is my personal approach that creates the climate. It is my daily mood that makes the weather. As a teacher I possess tremendous power to make a child's life miserable or joyous. I can be a tool of torture or an instrument of inspiration. In all situations it is my response that decides whether a crisis will be escalated or de-escalated, and a child humanized or de-humanized." [Ginott Intro]

All teachers hope, as they face a new group of students in September, that this year's crop will develop a cohesiveness, a group identity where caring and mutual support will prevail. Teachers want their classrooms to hum with the sounds of cooperation. Transforming a classroom into a place where students can risk failure takes time and care, yet all teachers know that the job of learning takes a back seat until trust has been established.

The following is a list of ideas and techniques used by teachers concerned with enhancing self-esteem and building a caring environment. I use these techniques in my classroom and I find that many are also applicable at home.

■ Teachers work with the children to develop a sense of pride within the class for the kind of behavior they all want to see developed.
■ Teachers establish with the children the rules and standards for their classroom.

- Teachers model respectful behavior and expect it in return. They comment when children show respect for others.
- Teacher emphasize how kids hurt or help each other by the comments they make.
- Teachers report to the class the compliments they have received from visitors and other teachers for their fine behavior.
- Teachers, knowing that the sum of the whole depends on each little part, establish a special relationship with each child, using private conversation, pats and thumbs-up, etc.
- Teachers use silent, secret signals for particular children to warn them about their behavior and praise them for compliance.
- Teachers may put up "traffic lights" to indicate expected behavior, i.e., a yellow light means that quiet talk and moving around the room is limited; red light means no talking.
- Teachers model a quiet working atmosphere by consistently maintaining an easygoing, unperturbed, manner.
- Teachers accept each opinion in a discussion, taking care not to evaluate opinions as though they were right or wrong.
- Teachers are careful to communicate instructions so everyone understands, even the shy or the slow-to-catch-on child.
- Teachers set aside a time towards the end of the day to evaluate how well the class members have followed their own rules, and to encourage everyone to express appreciation.

BE A KID ADVOCATE!

As parents you can help to create a positive environment in your child's school by giving of your time and interest, and by being supportive. Being supportive means attending each Back-to-School Night, Open House, and other parent meetings planned for your benefit. Being supportive means keeping abreast of what is being taught, discussing objectives with the teacher, and helping at home to meet those objectives.

Being supportive means becoming an advocate for kids. Ask questions about educational issues in your community, read any and all information available. If you don't understand some aspects of the school program, ask about them. Armed with the facts, parents can be among the most persuasive supporters of kids.

CREATING THE CLIMATE AT HOME

Even though teachers work with your children some four to six hours each day, the homefront is where the optimum opportunity for positive influence occurs. You, as parents, have twice the impact on a child's self-esteem as do teachers; you're the preventers of failure and the providers of success.

But establishing the best possible environment at home certainly does not happen with a snap of the fingers. And although we have all tried to glean the best techniques and strategies used by our own parents, we find that many of the old methods don't work.

IN THE "OLDEN DAYS"

In the past, two kinds of home environments have consistently failed to be effective in raising children with high self-esteem: 1) autocratic environments, and 2) permissive environments. In an autocratic environment, strict rules are rigidly enforced in a punitive manner. In a permissive environment, rules, if they exist, are lax and enforced inconsistently. Adults who were raised in these two environments frequently produce children with low self-esteem.

To their credit, wise parents have devised an alternative approach referred to as Democratic Parenting, the self-esteem building approach recommended in this book. As a introduction to the democratic approach, let's first examine how autocratic and permissive approaches evolved.

THE AUTOCRATIC APPROACH TO PARENTING

The autocratic approach for school and home dictates: "These are the rules by which you must abide. Violate them and you will be punished. By no means will children be involved in the decision-making process." It is doubtful that you are old enough to remember when the most important word in a family was OBEDIENCE, when wife obeyed husband and kids obeyed strict rules. In the school setting, children sat in straight rows and did their work obediently under the sharp eye of a solemn-faced disciplinarian. One hundred years ago it was probably a lot easier to be a teacher. He or she could say "Write!" and thirty pens would dip into inkwells. For years, children were reared and schooled according to the strict autocratic methods of their elders.

Parents using an autocratic parenting style have wondered why their children fail to develop a sense of responsibility. Research tells us that children subjected to the humiliating "Do it because I said so" methods do not learn to be in charge of themselves. When parents constantly take the responsibility for children's behavior, children do not become responsible.

THE PERMISSIVE APPROACH

In recent years many parents have swung from the autocratic approach to the other extreme: permissiveness, in part because they are disillusioned with their own parents' style. In this approach there are often no rules, limits or structure, or if there are rules they change constantly. Permissive parents say, in essence, "You can do anything you want to," resulting in mothers pleading

when they want a job done (clothes picked up from the floor) and then giving up after listening to children whining (and picking up the clothes themselves). A sense of responsibility is not engendered in this household either, for in a permissive environment no one takes responsibility. Children in these families sense a lack of order and feel insecure, confused and not taken care of.

You know parents who use one or the other of the preceding approaches with their children and some who have tried both at one time or another. They can all give you reasons, accompanied by examples, why neither method is effective in developing a cooperative atmosphere.

A DEMOCRATIC APPROACH

Research shows that students raised in an environment with well-defined limits develop positive self-esteem. So it would seem sensible for parents to consider the third leadership style, which I call Democratic Parenting, that promotes trust, freedom with order, and respect. Using this approach, parents:

- encourage independence
- listen
- allow for flexibility
- encourage risking
- trust their children
- keep promises
- invite children to help plan
- encourage change
- offer children choices
- promote cooperation
- keep rules to a minimum
- encourage responsibility

Democratic Parenting employs four major strategies to create this success-building climate.

- Build a backbone of trust.
- Set up negotiable rules.
- Offer limited choices.
- Spend time and tune in..

1) Build a Backbone of Trust

Double scoops of trust are required to build a desirable climate. Trust is the foundation of psychological security, the safe feeling a child needs in order to risk. The greater the sense of trust, the less the child needs to be guarded, withdrawn or fearful.

Most of us can remember a childhood situation where a promise was broken. We can recall the disappointment and, if subsequent promises were broken, the beginnings of distrust. When promises are kept, children learn to hope, but when promises are continually broken, confidence in adults tends to be destroyed. Adults who are dependable and reliable can build trust in many ways:

- Don't make promises you can't keep.
- Tell children where you are going and when you'll return.
- Talk openly and honestly about your feelings.
- Let children know they can count on you.

Trusting is a two-way street. Be trustworthy yourself, and expect children to be trustworthy, too.

My children's Grandma Jessie always professed trust in my three kids. "No matter what Chuckie says," she would announce to anyone listening, "I always know he tells the truth." Because she expected it, Chuckie always spoke the truth (at least to his Grandma Jessie). Out of the expectation grew the behavior, and therein lay the key to trustworthiness which my mother, of course, had in her pocket all along. The value of building trust in your children is an unparalleled first step toward creating the climate you want. Such a climate allows a child to proudly say, "I am trustworthy, and I can be open and trusting of others."

2) Set Rules Cooperatively

A body of rules is a necessity in every family. Rules help children know what is expected of them and what their parents define as good behavior. Rules offer a method of organizing life in the family whereby all members can know what their own and others' responsibilities are. Most families have rules about chores to be done, times to come in from play and get ready for bed, and acceptable behavior with sisters and brothers.

In a democratic environment, rules are clear, concise and few. Rules are established cooperatively, and input is encouraged from all children, however small. Rules are negotiable and parents are available to discuss reasonable changes: "Mommy, I think my puppy is now old enough to sleep with me." "Dad, now that I'm a year older, I'd like to stay up till 9:30."

3) Offer Limited Choices

All children grow in self-confidence when they are offered choices. Using a democratic approach suggests that parents constantly offer choices, a practice that demonstrates respect for the child and thus builds self-esteem. Here is an example of a parent using limited choices with a child:

> **Mom**: "Jack, the hedge in the back needs to be watered. Would you like to do it now or before dinner?"
> **Jack**: "Aw, I'll do it before dinner."
> (Later that day dinner is on the table, the hedge is still dry as a bone, and Jack comes in to eat.)
> **Mom**: "Jack, you need to do your watering. Shall I put your dinner in the oven or leave it on the table for you?"

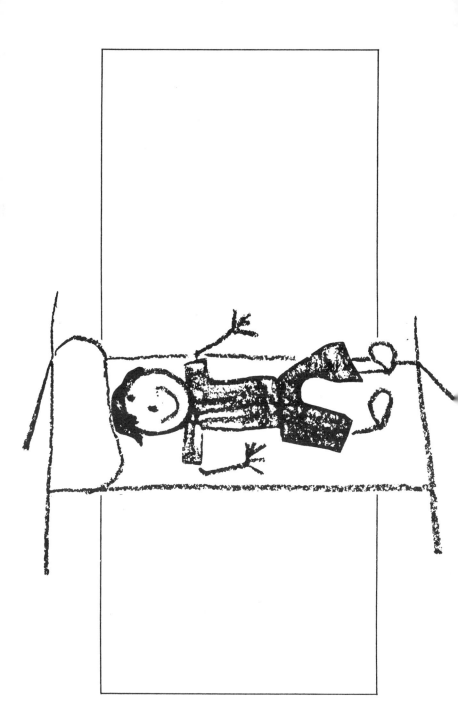

(Another choice. Now Jack either makes his decision about his food and goes out to do the watering or refuses to cooperate.) If there is no cooperation, here's the next choice:

Mom: "How long do you think you need to stay in your room, 10 minutes or 15?

(Let's say Jack spends 10 minutes in his room. His dinner is definitely less than tasty. Does Mom give in and serve it to him? Definitely not.)

Mom: "Your plate is still waiting till the job gets done, Jack. Shall I keep it in the oven or set it on the table?"

A child like Jack sooner or later comes to realize that this choice routine is going to prevail. Parents find that children respond to choices when they would not respond to demands. Choices give the child the feeling he or she is sharing the power. And a sense of power, we will discover, is one of the three essential components of self-esteem. In school, choices such as the following are deliberately offered to students:

"Students, here are assignments A, B, and C. Do them in whichever order you prefer."

"Choose the type of book report you prefer to do."

"Shall we make Friday the deadline or do you prefer Monday?"

Possible choices at home might be:

"Do you want to clean your room now or before your TV program?"

"Would you like to take the baby for a walk or do the dishes?"

Offering choices works wonders! Cooperation happens! Self-esteem is enhanced, kids feel better because they have a "say" in things, and parents marvel at the ease with which they accomplished it all.

4) Spend Time and Tune In

The fourth major strategy in a Democratic Parenting approach emanates from children themselves, many of whom wish for more time spent with their parents. I hear it from students when they say, "I like homework where my mom has to ask me the questions or say the spelling words," or "My favorite time is when my dad plays a game with me all alone."

What our children really want is time — more than they are getting now. Spending time says to the child, "I care about you. I want to spend time with you, to hear what's on your mind and what you're feeling. You are important to me."

I've heard valid excuses from working mothers and single parents who say they don't have enough time, and surely time is a scarce commodity to all of us. Nevertheless, experts agree that it's crucial, in today's fast-moving pace, to set aside regular, special time for each child. With young children it could be as little as 15 minutes a day, perhaps a walk around the block. With an older child it could be one hour a week, set aside for example, for a Sunday morning date at the pancake house. The important element is that the child can count on it.

In your time together, tune in to what your child is saying. Listen with full attention, whether he is describing his turn up at bat or sharing a problem at the bus stop. He doesn't need advice, pity, or your philosophical viewpoint. He needs someone to really listen and let him talk through his troubles or concerns. You don't have to say much, and often as not he will come to his own solutions.

PUT YOURSELF IN HIS SHOES

Imagine that you are this boy, Johnny, age 10. A lot of things worry you these days. You hear about them at school and see them on TV, and there's really nobody much around to talk to about it, since both your folks work all the time. You wish your dad had more time to spend with you; you wish your mom had more time to just talk; you wish you could discuss a few of your ideas and then just hang around together with your parents.

In *Childhood Stress*, Dr. Barbara Kuczen describes a ficticious young boy named Johnny, who lives in a home with two color TVs, a microwave oven and a personal computer. [pg. 205] He owns a 10-speed bike, and has been to Disneyworld twice. His parents, however, both work and he misses the family fun they had before the high cost of living took his mother back to full-time employment.

Perhaps this child, Johnny, sounds like someone you know. He is a good student and has learned in sixth grade about the energy crisis, the greenhouse effect, and the war in the Middle East. He has heard of artificial insemination and AIDS. He worries about what the future will be for his own children.

Dr. Kuczen states with tongue in cheek, "I wonder why a boy who has it so soft has ulcers."

Johnny is a child of a new age, and yet what is it that Johnny wishes for? Time spent with his parents! Boys and girls like Johnny go to school where I teach. I am sure they also attend your local school; perhaps they live in your house. Also attending our schools are children from less fortunate home situations. But whatever their advantages, many children are full of stress. Many feel like giving up; some feel suicidal. I hear of countless causes for stress, ranging from school difficulties and lack of friends to neighborhood violence and the threat of nuclear bombs.

What these children need is simple but crucial. They need to be listened to with empathy and understanding. They need to be encouraged to express opinions, make suggestions, and reach for solutions. They need to play and sing and laugh with you, their parents. They need the gift of your time.

If we believe, and there is plenty of evidence to believe, that having a sense of self-esteem will help keep kids out of trouble, then we have to feel that time spent with children is the best possible vaccine that democratic parents can use.

—■—

5

The Components of Self-Esteem

All people who have high self-esteem seem to possess certain characteristics that make them stand out and allow them to behave in certain ways:

1) They express confidence.
2) They act independently.
3) They express creativity and original ideas.
4) They seem to feel good about themselves.
5) They relate easily to others.
6) They work toward goals.
7) They are motivated to achieve.
8) They take risks.
9) They tolerate frustration well.

These characteristics can be categorized into three components of self-esteem. In this chapter, a brief description of these components provides an introduction to the succeeding three chapters in which they are described in depth. Recognizing children in terms of these components is very helpful toward developing confident, happy people, both tall and small.

The three components of self-esteem are:
■ a Sense of Connectedness
■ a Sense of Uniqueness
■ a Sense of Power

I sometimes refer to these components as ingredients in a cup of self-esteem. If a child has the three ingredients: C for Connectedness, U for Uniqueness, and P for Power, I say he has a full CUP.

A SENSE OF CONNECTEDNESS

A child with a sense of connectedness feels he or she belongs. This is a basic need for children as well as people of all ages. Kids need to feel they are part of a group, a family, a class, a student-body, a club or a team. They need to feel linked to others in an atmosphere of warm togetherness and good communication.

Conversely, some children feel that they never quite fit in. They lack a sense of connectedness. They may have difficulty making friends and so they spend a lot of time alone. They may turn to misbehavior to get the attention they need. These are children whose sense of connectedness needs boosting.

A SENSE OF UNIQUENESS

Children with a solid sense of uniqueness respect themselves. They celebrate their individuality, do their own thinking and express their own thoughts. They are confident. A sense of uniqueness is also a basic need of children.

On the other hand, some children don't feel special. Lacking a sense of uniqueness, they are likely to be followers who conform to the ideas of others, truly convinced that their opinions are of lesser value. Some, in a desperate bid to be unique in one way or another, choose to misbehave. Parents and teachers can recognize these children and help them raise their sense of uniqueness.

A SENSE OF POWER

Children who consider their choices and make their own decisions are children with a high sense of power. They feel they are in charge of their lives and can effect change. They are willing to try new things, meet challenges and take risks. They welcome responsibility and often develop strong leadership qualities.

Conversely, some children, lacking confidence, are afraid of failing and give up easily. These children, who have a low sense of power, have difficulty making decisions; they avoid taking responsibility and instead let others do things for them. These are children whose parents and teachers can help them build a sense of power.

QUICK IDENTIFICATION OF PROBLEM BEHAVIORS

Low Sense of Connectedness
- Communicates reluctantly
- Spends much time alone
- Has few friends
- Doesn't know how to relate
- Often acts silly
- Retreats to a favorite toy
- Keeps hurts to himself

Low Sense of Uniqueness
- Does not seem to feel "special"
- Mimics others
- Follows, conforms
- Shows off inappropriately
- Brags or boasts frequently
- Displays poor sportsmanship
- Chronically misbehaves

Low Sense of Power
- Fears failing
- Avoids risks and challenges
- Possesses poor academic skills
- Gives up easily
- Avoids taking responsibility
- Whines and blames
- Inveigles others to do his work

6

A Sense of Connectedness

When Michelle walks into the classroom each morning, she feels that she really belongs there; she's a part of the group; she's accepted and wanted. Michelle knows that the kids like her and miss her when she's absent. This secure feeling is called "a sense of connectedness." I once wrote a little poem about a child like Michelle:

I feel connected, I'm part of a team.
I'm important to people and I belong.
When I talk others listen, my opinion is heard.
It makes me feel secure and I am loved.

At home Michelle feels cherished. She knows she is an important member of the family whose opinion is taken into consideration. Because she feels loved at home and at school her self-esteem is constantly being increased.

THE NEED TO BELONG

A sense of connectedness, sometimes referred to as a feeling of belonging, is a basic need in all of us beginning at a young age. Children need to be a part of a group, a team, or a club, and that need increases as they approach adolescence, when acceptance by peers becomes an even more vital concern. Teenagers go to great lengths to be a part of the group in their dress, hairstyle, verbal expression, and behavior. It is often the lack of acceptance in a socially appropriate group that motivates participation in gangs. A young person will find acceptance in one environment or another.

So it is with all of us. Adults also need to feel we're a part of a family, a neighborhood, a work crew, perhaps a class we're taking or a committee on which we participate. Through our relationships with others we see the reflections of our opinions of ourselves, our self-concepts. If our relationships are basically positive, that is, if we feel appreciated and liked, then our self-esteem grows. If our relationships are basically negative, our self-esteem becomes shaky and emotional development is blocked. If we are frequently hurt or rejected, we may turn to isolation or to self-destructive behavior, decisions that we make subconsciously.

Mother Teresa, the Nobel Peace Prize-winning nun who devoted her life to tending the poor and sick in the slums of Calcutta, once stated, "In these years of work among the people, I have come more and more to realize that being unwanted is the worst disease any human being can experience."

Can a sense of connectedness be rehabilitated in teenagers who have chosen gang membership and other self-destructive behavior? Can we, as adults, turn the tide of our own isolation or destructiveness and rebuild a sense of connectedness? Can we overcome past experiences that were hurtful and damaging? The answer is a resounding "Yes!" It is never too late to begin!

Like most tasks, building a sense of connectedness is easier if it is begun early in life. Teachers know this. A preschool teacher watches a sense of connectedness begin to form as she encourages a three-year-old to join a small play group. Elementary school teachers realize that children need to feel like responsible members of the group while maintaining their own uniqueness, so they design curriculum that includes cooperative group assignments.

BEHAVIOR RELATED TO A HIGH SENSE OF CONNECTEDNESS

The opening words of this chapter described the feelings of a girl named Michelle, who had a high sense of connectedness. She felt accepted and cherished. We can also describe a child with a high sense of connectedness in terms of behavior, using adjectives like outgoing, extroverted, and friendly. I refer to such a child as a "High C Kid."

The behavior of a High C Kid in school is shown by an eagerness to be a part of things, by listening, contributing, and regularly participating. When working in a small group this child assumes an equal portion of the responsibility, not by pushing or promoting himself, but by doing his part.

We can pick out High C Kids on any playground. They're involved. They have something going, and quite likely they've been instrumental in the organization of the game. Teachers on the playground note the friendliness of High C Kids. They report that High C Kids look you in the eye; they greet you with a "Hi, Mrs. Johnson. You sure look nice today!"

Adults like these kids; we connect with them and find ourselves smiling as we pass by, perhaps even envying their easy nonchalance. Social graces seem to come so naturally to High C children.

The child's behavior at home is also a reflection of his or her feelings. He who feels he truly belongs takes part in conversations, shows concern for big sister's problems and interest in little brother's activities. Being an integral part of the family is important and a child's behavior reflects it.

CLUES TO A LOW SENSE OF CONNECTEDNESS

The feelings as well as the behavior of a Low C Kid are significantly different than those of the child described

above. Many people react to misbehavior without really looking at its underlying implications. Perhaps we try but become frustrated. And surely, understanding the reasons for behavior is not easy, since it involves getting underneath to the feelings. But it is vitally important to first understand the feelings of a Low C Kid, and then take a closer look at his or her behavior. To aid understanding, I once wrote a little poem about a child with a low sense of connectedness:

> *People don't like me, I feel I don't belong.*
> *So I hide inside my jacket and don't let on how I hurt.*
> *I bug you for attention; I'll get it good or bad.*
> *Nobody plays with me, but I just say I don't care.*

PUT YOURSELF IN HIS SHOES

You are a Low C Kid named Timmy. At recess you burst out the door with the rest of the class. You watch as the others run off toward the playground and you wonder, "How do they always know just the right, 'rad' words to shout at each other? And why don't they ask me to play? How come I never seem to fit in?"

You're afraid that you are different, or just not likeable. So you try to decide what to do. "Shall I go play with the kindergartners? Shall I hang around and talk to the teacher? Or should I try once more to join the gang on the basketball court?"

You lean on the fence watching until the bell rings. Another recess is over, and you slowly trudge back to the classroom. Your sadness makes your tummy hurt.

Children with a low sense of connectedness feel uncomfortable in almost any group. With the kids on the playground they feel not quite wanted; in the neighborhood they may feel accepted but not really sought after. In the classroom, where the other kids all seem to belong, Low C Kids feel they are on the outside.

Can you empathize with Timmy and recognize his low self-esteem? He is experiencing loneliness and rejection and he wonders what's wrong with him. Now the question is: What will be Timmy's resulting behavior? If this were you, standing on the playground feeling left out, or sitting dejectedly in a class where you don't seem to fit in, how would you react?

There are two categories of behavior that Low C Kids exhibit as a result of their feelings. We learned earlier that a "Low C adult" turns either to isolation or to self-destructive behavior. So it will not be surprising to find that Low C Kids react either by 1) withdrawal or 2) acting out. Let's examine the behavior of each reaction category very closely.

REACTION BEHAVIOR (1) WITHDRAWAL

The child who chooses withdrawal:
- spends much of his or her time alone
- is uncomfortable about hugging or touching
- avoids eye contact
- shrugs off rejection by the group
- carries little toys in his pocket to play with
- may relate closely to a pet
- may interact with very young children
- constantly wears a favorite sweatshirt or jacket
- avoids talking about feelings

Please keep in mind that all children will act in these ways sometimes, since we all have occasions to feel less "connected." We need to look for patterns and frequency of the behaviors. If a child acts in the ways listed above on a continual basis, we conclude that he has a low sense of connectedness.

This child, feeling uncomfortable in almost any group, chooses to spend a lot of time alone. He or she may have a private fort out behind the garage or a "nest" in the bedroom. (I once peeked into a special cave in a bedroom closet, complete with reading light and a full array of snacks.) These retreats give comfort to a Low C Kid.

Wanting friends desperately, these children may nevertheless behave like they couldn't care less. "Who needs 'em?" they declare. They sorely need to be accepted and liked, but constant rejection has caused a calloused attitude.

Caring parents consistently ask, "What happened in school today?" They know the importance of showing interest and keeping communication channels open. Think back to Timmy, our Low C Kid on the playground. How likely is he to relate his feelings to his mom? Will he tell her he wonders what's wrong with him? Not likely. This child is a "Cover-up Kid," remember? While most kids will share a few tidbits of information about their day, the Cover-up Kid will not. And if he mumbles a few words about one of the day's events, undoubtedly he will omit any mention of hurt feelings.

Have you noticed that some kids avoid eye contact, and are uncomfortable about being touched? It's hard to get a hug from a child with a stiff back and a "stay away" attitude. Have you noticed kids who, avoiding people, relate easily to animals or prefer playing with preschoolers? Most likely these are kids with a low sense of connectedness.

Teachers have observed that some children prefer to wear their jackets in class all the time, hot days and cool. I had a boy named Jay who constantly wore a striped cap that came down around his ears. I know that cap felt comforting on Jay's head. I also know why Kevin wore his jacket all day, and kept a minimum of three little cars in his pocket. Jay and Kevin felt lonely sitting there not connected with anyone. Like a cap or a jacket, favorite toys can be a comfort as a child deals with loneliness.

REACTION BEHAVIOR (2) ACTING OUT

The child who chooses to act out:
- tries to copy other kids' behavior
- bugs everybody in search of attention
- is pushy, bossy and aggressive
- teases smaller children
- interrupts other kids' games
- perseveres in an inexhaustible amount of inappropriate behavior

The children in the second category choose more overt methods of dealing with a low sense of connectedness. They begin by closely observing the social interactions of others in their neighborhood or school playground in order to emulate the behavior. Watching others relate, they fail to realize, however, that successful give-and-take interaction skills take several years to learn and are refined by much practice. Our Low C Kids try to copy what they see and hear, an admirable idea but very difficult to carry off. Almost always they fail. Their attempts to imitate appear silly and contrived. Sadly enough, the attempts usually result in their being ridiculed, shunned or ignored by the other kids.

Children who choose the withdrawal behavior as previously described give up when shunned by peers. But these "acting-out" kids persevere. In their inept way they become aggressive and pushy; they demand attention in a never-ending array of inappropriate behavior.

As we can all testify, children who demand attention

turn people off and frustrate all of us. They become known as the neighborhood pests and the classroom troublemakers. Interestingly enough, these labels spur them to greater levels of excellence in this role. They become expert at being pests: they talk loudly and act bossy; they tease little kids; they insist on being first.

Such children do get attention, but it comes in negative forms: 1) put-downs from the peer group and 2) reprimands from adults. They do connect with others but the connections are counter-productive. None of the attention they receive is the accepting, nurturing kind that they so desperately need.

BUILDING A SENSE OF CONNECTEDNESS AT SCHOOL

Most readers must be wondering, "What can possibly be done to help a child who has become so discouraged that he or she either acts out or withdraws and gives up?" Teachers wonder too, and they struggle for answers. Requests for help from the Office of Education result in directives delivered to teachers' desks:

1) Promote affiliation and acceptance.
2) Encourage peer support and approval.
3) Increase awareness.

Excellent ideas in theory, but leaving the practicalities to the classroom teacher, who must then search his or her files and years of experience for workable techniques and "how-to's."

Teachers realize the crucial need to belong that is felt by students. We look around at the 30 faces in our classrooms, and by the second week of school we can make dozens of salient observations about the levels of connectedness. For example:

■ Kim does not contribute to a discussion unless called upon; she avoids all eye contact.

- Jason and Ellie are not participating in their small group projects.
- Kevin has worn his zip-up sweatshirt all day for a week, sometimes with the hood up.
- Chris is constantly turning classmates off with his inappropriate remarks.
- Antonio plays alone at recess.
- Randy tries to buy friendship with little toys.

What is to be done? Where does a teacher begin? How can she possibly meet the needs of Kim, Kevin, Antonio and the others who are already beginning to slip through the cracks? How will she find the time as she concentrates on reading, math and the seven other curriculum areas?

A good teacher always begins, as we have learned, by creating a caring environment. His or her goal is that every child will feel accepted and wanted. With that goal in mind the good teacher infuses love into every lesson, be it math or music, spelling or science.

Within the caring environment, a variety of techniques are implemented to build a sense of connectedness. In addition to their main purpose, these techniques also:

- increase interest in learning
- enhance motivation
- improve behavior
- build basic values such as kindness and cooperation
- develop critical thinking
- lead to higher test scores
- make learning more enjoyable

CLASSROOM TECHNIQUES

I. Cooperative Learning Strategies

"I create situations where kids can work in pairs," reports one teacher. "Spelling was never meant to be studied alone." Working together with one other classmate is an excellent connectedness-building experience for a Low C Kid, and a first step to other activities that involve groups of three or more.

These carefully structured groups, also referred to as study groups, cooperative learning groups, or Tribes, allow children to collaborate on such activities as research, art projects, math games, and report-writing. Students are encouraged to evaluate each cooperative learning activity when it is completed, and give helpful comments to their fellow group members.

II. Concept Circles and Classroom Meetings

Many teachers regularly conduct a circle discussion with all class members, in which children are encouraged to share feelings and thoughts and/or solve problems brought forward by members of the class. Courteous listening habits and acceptance of everyone's opinion are emphasized; this builds respect for likenesses and differences of all.

Whereas the main goal of this activity is to build self-awareness, wise teachers observe the sense of security that grows when children realize 1) that their comments will be accepted unconditionally, and 2) that everyone has the right to pass. Teachers with wonderful patience and perseverance give a smile and a thumbs-up to each child, those who contribute as well as those who pass.

III. Praise and Reinforcement

Good teachers give feedback to their Low C students who interact successfully with another. Even in preschool, when a teacher observes successful partner play, he or she reinforces the newly-developing skills. "You divided those blocks to make it fair for both of you, Kenny. That's called cooperation!"

IV. Dispensing Love In The Classroom

Teachers plan outdoor games where nobody is a loser, and contests where everyone wins. They distribute smiles, winks, and pats on the back. They make every attempt, in their busy day to give quality time just listening.They endeavor to create a special, very personal relationship with any child whom they perceive to have a low sense of connectedness. Teachers are the possessors of patience, and the donors of acceptance and love.

THE ORIGINS OF CONNECTEDNESS

Do you remember Michelle, the High C Kid we met at the beginning of this chapter? We found that Michelle's behavior reflected her strong feelings of belonging. Long before Michelle began kindergarten her sense of connectedness began to develop, promoted by her parents. This

PUT YOURSELF IN HER SHOES

You are a two-year-old. You can't tell the grown-ups that what you really want is to be recognized as a big kid and an important member of the family. So you say, "No! Me do it!"

What you're really saying is, "Here I am! Pay attention! I pull some weight in this family, too! I want to be treated like I belong here. I am developing my sense of connectedness." Your way of saying all that is "NO!" And does it ever feel good to be assertive!

was obvious to Michelle's first teachers. What is not always so obvious is just how this sense of connectedness evolves.

A child is not born with a sense of connectedness, but almost immediately after birth he or she begins to respond and relate. He very rapidly develops certain techniques for interacting with others: smiling, laughing out loud, crying and yelling, patting mama's cheek and pulling daddy's ear. In these moments a sense of connectedness, either high or low, first begins to be built. According to the responses given the child by parents, he or she becomes either friendly and outgoing or uncomfortable around others.

Another series of events begin to occur as a baby approaches the toddler stage. During this period, in which child psychologists tell us a child's primary assignment in life is to assert herself, she begins to take on the world face-to-face. Down go the heels, out goes the chin, and the "No's" flow fast and furiously. The flag of independence is raised, and parents can be observed, mouths open, in a state of shock.

Dealing with a two-year-old seeking independence presents an excellent opportunity for parents to build self-esteem. This stretch for independence and inclusion must be respected as merely the first of many stretches.

A child's sense of connectedness now begins to be molded by the quality of the interpersonal relations in the family, and the opportunities to interact that are provided. Wise parents keep in mind their child's basic need to be an integral part of 1) the family and 2) the peer group.

HOW PARENTS BUILD A SENSE OF CONNECTEDNESS

1) Coordinate events that require the help of every family member to plan, cook and prepare, with everyone working together to pull it off.

2) Encourage family members to share feelings, interests, and personal matters with each other.

3) Insure that everyone in the family has a full share of weekly chores and responsibilities, using a job list if it is helpful.

4) Let everyone voice an opinion on family plans of great importance, such as choosing paint for the bathroom, building a deck, or taking a weekend trip.

5) Help your children build friendships, and teach them how to be good friends. Discuss together the damage that can be done by gossiping, breaking promises or being unfair. Point out the lasting advantages of a good friendship.

6) Make your home available to your children's friends; provide a welcoming atmosphere. This is a practice that really pays off in the long run. When you encourage your children to let their friends "hang out" at your home, they receive a message from you which says, "I trust your judgment in friendships. I believe in you and welcome your friends here." Few children, feeling this powerful message, will damage that trust.

7) Encourage children to join a scout troupe, a club, a church group, a gymnastics team, or any kids' group in your community. My daughter Susan's sense of connectedness was greatly enhanced when she joined our local swim team and was required to attend daily practices. Of all the benefits Susan realized, one of the greatest was the chance to build lasting friendships with boys of her own age.

8) Actively support the groups they join; give of your interest and enthusiasm and of your time. Be involved in their activities: throw the ball, measure a long jump, applaud a dance step, adjust a handlebar. When they see you taking an interest, they feel loved.

Part of building connectedness is accepting your

children as they are. This requires taking them seriously. The things that happen in your children's lives are of tremendous importance to them. Show your interest. Kids who grow up in a family with an autocratic approach to parenting have a distinct handicap in that they are taught, "Children should be seen and not heard." Their self-esteem suffers when they are deprived of the opportunity to express their thoughts and opinions. Many of them come to believe that their thoughts aren't important. Really listen to your kids.

Use "door openers" that invite children to say more about an incident or explain their feelings: "I see," "Oh," "Tell me more," "No kidding," "Say that again, I want to be sure I heard you." Give your undivided attention when your children need to talk to you.

You can show interest in little children by hunkering down to their level. Look them in the eye and really listen. Go off to a quiet place with your older child to talk. Get into his shoes and try to understand what he means. Let him finish; don't interrupt; try not to be thinking of what you are going to say next.

An old friend whose children were grown once advised me to try the "Mmm" technique. It concerns the responses we give to children with whom we want to maintain open communication. The "Mmm" technique sounds like this:

Daughter: "Mom, my friend Stacy got grounded for a whole month."
Mom: "Mmm?"
Daughter: "Don't you think it's unfair? The only thing Stacy did was smoke."
Mom: "Mmm."
Daughter: "She didn't even buy the pot. Somebody gave it to her."
Mom: "Mmm!"

Daughter: "Come to think of it, Mom, I guess Stacy really made a bad choice."
Mom: "Mmm!"

A mother/daughter exchange such as this one can be a lead-up to a compatible, constructive discussion. This wise mother knew when to keep quiet. She also foresaw the detrimental results of responses such as (a) censorship of Stacy, (b) concurrence with Stacy's parents, or (c) a lecture. Communication would have been severed. It's often better just to listen and wait, for when we really listen we build trust and closeness. Then self-esteem increases. It's also helpful to use responses such as "You may be right," "I never thought of it that way," or "You have a point," in order to show acceptance. Then self-esteem increases.

A wise grandmother once advised me, "Love your children enough to let them go." Wisdom indeed, because independence must be encouraged. I think we all know the damage that can be done by a clutching parent. Love is trusting, cherishing, encouraging, and many splendored things that build a sense of connectedness. And then love is letting them go.

A Sense of Uniqueness

"Does anyone know the definition of the word hydraulics"? asks Mr. D., who is introducing a new concept to his students. One hand shoots up immediately. "Yes, Michael, do you know the meaning?" "Well, no, not exactly, but I think hydro means water," suggests Michael, "so hydraulics might be some kind of water operation."

Mr. D. could have predicted that a hypothesis would come from Michael. Here is a child who is unique in his willingness to venture a guess. Michael trusts his own perceptions and feels confident in his theories. In addition, he is willing to risk being wrong. Michael has what we call "a sense of uniqueness." I once wrote a little poem about a child like Michael:

> *I'm somebody special and I'm unique.*
> *I use my imagination in my very own way.*
> *I have my own style, I express my own self,*
> *I like being different because I am me!*

BEHAVIOR RELATED TO A HIGH SENSE OF UNIQUENESS

"High U Kids" are usually leaders who express their own opinions. They trust their personal reactions and intuition. They believe in themselves and this belief allows them to carry out their unique ideas. These are the trendsetters who come to school with an original combination of wearing apparel, or a new game they've invented. These are the originators of clubs and the idea-men (and women) for new school projects. These are creative kids.

All of this creativity has been encouraged by the

parents of these children — even the rad, fantastic expressions. Children with a solid sense of uniqueness have learned to respect and value themselves because they have been respected and valued at home. Parents have listened to their opinions and have taken them seriously. High U Kids know that others consider them special by the way they are treated. Teachers like them for their cleverness; peers clamor for their company, and grandpas' chests swell with pride.

Kids vary as to the attributes that they consider special. Children who are very capable intellectually may place little value on their abilities and wish to be socially popular or athletic instead. Others may wish for the ability to learn things easily. A child may feel that his or her uniqueness is:

- an ability in sports — he or she is a fast runner or a good diver, etc.
- a talent — he or she plays the drum or can draw scenery.
- appearance — he or she looks clean and neat, dresses nicely.
- knowledge — he or she is an "expert" on dinosaurs or airplanes.
- a special skill — he or she can handle tools, write stories, or organize projects.
- a physical ability — he or she can do karate, dance or gymnastics.
- sensitivity — he or she is thoughtful and empathic toward others.

The list is endless, because every one of us is unique. In the words of a favorite song sung in my classroom: "I'm a special person — I'm out of sight!"

I once asked a group of nine-year-olds to write down their "specials." The list included: master fisherman, excellent at remembering jokes, and expert pancake-maker. What wonders kids are, and how predictably unpredictable!

I have observed children with a high sense of uniqueness in school. To my delight I have repeatedly found one marvelous common quality: an accepting, noncompetitive attitude toward others. As they recognize their own strengths and skills, they also recognize the special abilities of others. As they feel secure in their social relationships, they put themselves out to be open, friendly and willing to share. When a good idea pops into Michael's head, he wants to share it immediately and get feedback from a friend. He takes pride in his successes and wants others to succeed also. No wonder teachers like these children — they serve as models to help us build self-esteem in others!

A sense of uniqueness, sometimes referred to as a feeling of significance, is basic to positive growth in all of us. We need to feel that within the family, the classroom, or any group, we have an important role that is significant in the eyes of others. We need the attention and recognition that it brings.

CLUES TO A LOW SENSE OF UNIQUENESS

Sadly enough, many children feel that nothing about them is special; they have no qualities nor abilities worth mentioning. They are unsure of their strengths or whether for certain they do have positive characteristics. In addition, they may be uncomfortable with their physical appearance and label themselves "ugly." They may feel inadequate as a learner ("stupid"), or unacceptable socially ("a nerd").

I once wrote a poem for a child with a low sense of uniqueness:

I'm nobody special so I follow someone else.
I'm very easily influenced, my confidence is low.

I mimic other kids, I'm embarrassed to be me,
Or I show off and misbehave in any way I can.

Obviously these children are not receiving the positive attention or recognition from others that is a basic need of everyone. Perhaps no one at home seems to consider them unique; perhaps no adults have helped them discover their special qualities. Since a sense of uniqueness is basic to emotional growth, how can we begin to help these children?

Children with a low sense of uniqueness come in two varieties: 1) the followers and 2) the misbehavers. Both seek recognition and attention. Recognizing the behavior

PUT YOURSELF IN HER SHOES

Suppose that you are a girl named Sherrie. During reading time your thoughts are wandering. "I'm glad I wore my new tennies today because Jennie and Amy are wearing theirs, and now they'll notice me. Maybe they'll let me play with them at recess. I wonder what we'll play — I'd rather we all play jumprope but I'll just have to wait for them to decide."

You suddenly realize that everyone else in class is finishing their assignments. As you hurry to finish you have one last thought about recess that brings a small pang of regret. It's about your friend Linda. "Of course we won't play with Linda because Jenny and Amy say they don't like her."

of each will aid in understanding the feelings that are so hurtful.

1. NOBODY SPECIAL: THE FOLLOWER.

Sherrie is a follower who constantly conforms to the ideas of others. Sherrie needs attention and recognition but, rarely trusting her own opinions, copies someone else. In a class discussion, she repeats another child's comments. Sherrie seems not to have developed the confidence to use her own imagination; she rarely contributes original ideas.

A child with a low sense of uniqueness checks with peers to know what to do, when to laugh, what to wear, and what and whom to like or dislike. A Low U Kid like Sherrie constantly checks with others for approval.

Sherrie carefully avoids being a stand-out; she wants to look good within the confines of looking like everyone else. Such a child, when a little older, will choose the hair style, make-up, nail polish etc. that is currently "in." A Low U Kid is reluctant to risk looking or acting different; in fact, risking is something rarely done at all.

I had a student named Jaime who constantly spoke negatively of himself. Whenever he brought a work paper or a drawing to my desk he would say, "This is probably wrong, Mrs. Reider." Jaime would put himself down on any occasion. His sense of uniqueness was so low that he was truly convinced that very little of what he did was of value.

2. NOBODY SPECIAL: THE MISBEHAVER

Carl chooses another way to behave in order to get the attention and recognition he needs. Although Carl also believes he is nobody special, he chooses not to be a follower but instead to misbehave. It is necessary for parents and teachers to thoroughly understand a child like Carl.

As we have said, every child (and every adult) needs attention and recognition. If a child doesn't have these needs met, he or she very often makes an unconscious decision to misbehave, in a bid for attention. It is important to remember that the decision is made unconsciously.

Carl seeks attention by constantly interrupting with smart, braggadocio comments. If the teacher holds up a book to read to the class, Carl is the kind of child who blurts out, "Aw, we've got that on video!" When another child tells about his toy or bike, Carl is apt to brag, "My bike's more rad than his!"

Here is a child with a very low sense of uniqueness. He is saying, in effect, "I have no special qualities, so in order to get attention, I misbehave. My misbehavior (interrupting) is my special ability; I have become an expert at it and each time you reprimand me that specialness is confirmed."

Yes, a kid like Carl is reprimanded. He expects it but does nothing about curbing his misbehavior. And many children are just like Carl, although one may choose to be a show-off, a class clown, or a fighter. If fighting becomes a child's specialty, and that specialty is confirmed with attention, then even though that attention is punishment, the child is unlikely to stop fighting.

Tony was the class clown and one of the most clever 10-year-old comedians I ever knew. He could pull an instant pun at any occasion; his constant remarks made the students fall apart laughing. Although I appreciated Tony's wit, his interruptions soon got out of hand and became rude and uncalled-for. Tony's self-esteem was shaky and he craved attention, so cracking jokes became his specialty.

Carl and Tony are misbehavers with tenacity, not unlike the kid who brags, "Aha! I'm the worst kid in class!" And spends his time proving it.

Professional counselors who work with children

realize that these children have such a strong need for a sense of uniqueness that they will settle upon negative characteristics as special. In truth, both Carl and Tony would prefer to be recognized by parents, teachers, or peers for appropriate behavior, but no such positive recognition is forthcoming. So they turn to misbehavior.

Teachers, in their frustration, often seek help from a school counselor. Such a professional, working with either of these boys would lead him to understand the reasons for his behavior and the steps he could take to change it. Even very young children have been helped to understand that all kids need attention and sometimes act out in order to get it.

Trained counselors aren't the only people who can deal with misbehavers like these, however. Parents and teachers can do wonders with Low U Kids, even though they are the biggest troublemakers and the most exasperating children we know. The only requirements on our part are large amounts of patience and willingness to spend the time.

No single component among the three in our full cup is more significant than any other, although a sense of uniqueness is the most rewarding to build. Let's examine the techniques of a skillful teacher first, then follow with democratic parenting strategies.

BUILDING A SENSE OF UNIQUENESS AT SCHOOL

Since long before October, Mr. D. has been aware of the variety of behaviors being exhibited in his classroom. He notices that Sherrie allows other girls to make decisions for her which causes deeper unhappiness. He is completely exasperated with Carl's rude interruptions.

Aside from these two who need his immediate attention, Mr. D. observes several others in his class whose behavior denotes a shaky sense of uniqueness:

- Roy keeps a constant eye on the class cut-up, and laughs whenever a disturbance is created.
- Carmen and John rarely, if ever, make original comments in a discussion.
- Anthony has been instigating arguments that threaten to cause playground fights.
- Miguel and Timmy are both borrowing answers from other students' papers.
- Tom's work is not being done, and he's becoming a show-off.

These children all feel inadequate in school and therefore have adapted some form of defensive behavior. Others may act defiant, sullen, or silly as a means of avoiding the issue. Some may appear to be distracted, unmotivated or negative. They may find some way to "cop out" rather than risk failure. All Cover-up Kids present a challenge to adults, at home and at school.

CLASSROOM TECHNIQUES

Teachers know that the child who is hardest to love is the one who needs it the most. To meet the challenge of cover-up behavior, they begin with acceptance of each and every child. They rely on intuition, inherent ability, and experience.

If I were to gather the techniques used by the teachers in any given school, the list would exceed one thousand. Good teachers are full of good ideas, many of which are also applicable at home.

1. Finding Their Uniqueness

Discover something about the Cover-up Kid that is special: a quality, a characteristic, a talent, trait or ability. A telling remark was made on a preceding page about Carl and Tony, our misbehavers. It stated that both boys would prefer positive recognition for their good qualities, if that were forthcoming. Carl and Tony know deep down that they aren't liked. There is no doubt in their minds as to their parents' anger and their teachers' frustration. But they also hold a deep down glimmer of hope that someday, somebody will recognize something good about them.

Mr. D., meanwhile, is also spending his recess at his desk. Chin in hand, he is contemplating three small signs tacked to his wall as he worries about Carl.

There is no such thing as a bad child, only discouraged.

Catch kids doing something good.

Find their uniqueness.

PUT YOURSELF IN HIS SHOES

You are an eight-year-old named Carl, and you are spending your recess in the classroom. Mr. D. has told you to think about your misbehavior toward Matt. You sit dejectedly at your desk, chin in hand. "Sure, I laughed when Matt made a mistake," you tell yourself. "And sure, I called him a nerd. But Matt won't play with me lately and that hurts my feelings. It's the same with all the guys — nobody likes me anymore. Mr. D. seems disgusted. I wish he knew how much I want kids to like me. I wish he would say nice things to me like he says to Matt. I hate Matt. No wonder I call him a nerd."

Mr. D. says to himself, "Look how Carl is acting in order to get some kind of recognition. What can I find about Carl that is commendable? How can I make a difference in this child's life?" By the time recess ends, Mr. D. has made these plans: 1) To ignore Carl's desperate bids for attention and 2) to catch him doing something good.

Mr. D.'s determination will help him discover qualities in Carl and other equally frustrating children if he is willing to persevere. If he searches diligently he will find hidden qualities in all children, such as:

- sense of humor
- courtesy to elderly persons
- empathy for the underdog
- willingness to help out in a crisis

Parents can help a teacher by suggesting special qualities exhibited at home but not readily obvious at school.

Besides personal qualities, hidden talents and abilities can also be discovered. Nobody knew about Carl's expertise at drawing cartoons and lettering captions until Mr. D. made the discovery. Perhaps he will commission Carl to illustrate the class booklet to be displayed at Open House, or ask him to be in charge of the caption for a bulletin board. Perhaps he will promote in Carl a willingness to cooperate that may decrease his need to disturb the class.

Some teachers consider the opportunity to discover and capitalize on a child's specialties one of their greatest privileges. It surely is one of our biggest challenges. Another of Mr. D.'s students named Justin had been bidding for attention by refusing to do his work. Recognizing real math potential in Justin, Mr. D. appointed him "math consultant." What a change came about in Justin when he found himself not only saluted for his math progress but a consultant for others. Justin soon had no need for negative strokes; he was receiving all he needed in appropriate ways.

2. Promote Self-Awareness

Since many children are not aware of their strengths, teachers think of ways to help kids discover what's good about themselves. Concept-circle discussions can help. (See Chapter VI) In these discussions, all opinions are valued and everyone has the right to pass. Good topics to build self-awareness are:

- Good things about me
- What I'm proud of
- What's important in my life
- Something that embarrasses me
- What makes me angry
- What I discovered I can do

Discussions often lead to writing assignments. Students display their illustrated compositions on the wall or compile them into booklets. Precious "ME BOOKLETS" can be made starting before kindergarten, with pictures and dictated captions.

3. Promote originality

To encourage creativity, teachers set out lots of science and art materials for experimentation. To encourage originality, teachers set up debates and applaud ideas that are different. To encourage individuality, teachers arrange for kids to achieve alone, so they can say, "I did it my way!"

Building a sense of uniqueness is a de facto item on school principals' job descriptions. They greet students by name, show interest in science projects, and promote young writers. They listen to beginning readers, encourage budding athletes, and discover hidden talents.

When she discovered that my son Chuck was a 10-year-old nouveau drummer, our school principal arranged a one-man concert. The entire student body arrived en masse to cheer and applaud. Imagine the self-esteem that was built that day!

HOW PARENTS BUILD A SENSE OF UNIQUENESS

As was pointed out in Chapter IV, children's self-esteem reflects the family climate. A family can establish an atmosphere that encourages a sense of uniqueness. The special feeling that is promoted at home is what children carry to the classroom. Parents can consider some of the following suggestions.

1. Model Self-Respect

You, mom, and you, dad, are unique in all this world; no one is exactly like you. You possess dignity; you are important and worthy of respect. You must show your children, through your behavior, that you respect yourself. When children see this, they will begin to adopt the attitude that they see modeled. Your behavior should include no self put-downs and no grumbling about your bad luck in life. It should include a willingness to risk and make changes, an acceptance of responsibility, and an attitude of confidence. Let your children see shining examples!

2. Applaud The Uniqueness of Your Child

Point out something unique or special about each of your children. Encourage them to express themselves in their own unique ways, and reinforce this uniqueness. Children who are encouraged to dance to their own music will have high levels of self-esteem.

The Bensons, who have four children attending our school, are very active in sports and encourage it in their children. Mom plays on an adult ball team; Dad loves all sports and the challenge of competition. Three of the Benson children are also sports enthusiasts, but Bob, the second-oldest, is different. He would rather fish than join the family when they go white-water rafting. He would rather time the swimmers than compete in the swim meet. His parents hold unrealistic expectations of Bob, so in order to please them he tries to be like the others. He signs up for teams but fails, and then is ashamed. As a result, he considers himself a failure. To Bob, his parents and siblings are successful and he is unworthy. He desperately needs to hear that being different is not wrong. He needs to have his interest in fishing encouraged; he needs to know that he is special in his own right. A parent's high expectations may do great damage to a child.

3. Survey Each Child With a Different View

No one likes to be compared with others. As an adult, you resent hearing, "You're not as clever as your brother." "Your hair was never as wavy as your sister's." The same applies to children, yet parents find it extremely difficult not to compare. Naturally, they see similar behaviors or

PUT YOURSELF IN HIS SHOES

A 10-year-old who feels grown-up, you are nevertheless the baby of the family and you hate it! You hear your dad talking to the soccer coach, "Funny how this kid doesn't get the hang of it; my older two were champs." You hear your mom on the phone to your grandma, "His grades are so much lower than his sister's when she was in fifth grade." The principal greets you with "Oh, you're one of the Jones kids. I hope you make the honor roll like the others did." Your anxiety rises. You know you can't live up to everything "they" did, so why even try? It's all so very discouraging.

characteristics in younger children and make comparisons.

Learn to avoid making comparisons, especially those accompanied by judgment. But more than simply avoiding comparisons, genuinely accept your children as unique persons. Love them for who are are and you will never hear in later years, "You always loved John better than me!"

4. Foster Creativity

Creativity is uniqueness. It is not limited to artistic or musical ability, but can be any activity we enjoy. Cooking dinner, building a bookshelf, even writing a good letter can be a creative enterprise.

Children with a high sense of uniqueness tend to see creative opportunities in the most ordinary places or things. They can turn a ruler into a magic wand, and a back yard into a jungle. All children are creative and we can encourage or discourage that creativity. It is our attitude as teachers and parents that fosters their instinctive creative impulses. It is our behavior and the messages we deliver that make the difference.

Consider some of the ways you speak to your children. Instead of "Just follow the directions on that toy set," say, "I wonder how many things you can think of to build." Instead of, "This is the way we've always done it in this family," say, "Let's hear your idea; maybe we can try another method." Instead of, "Can't you see things the way others do?" say, "Good for you for sticking to your point of view."

Creative children are intensely curious. Avoid ignoring or shrugging off their persistent questions; take as much time as you can to show your interest in their inquiries. Turn a "why" question back to the child with "Why do you think?" When riding in the car, Jilly at five was 1) extremely inquisitive and 2) eager for attention. "What's this button? What's that for?" Her patient auntie turned the questions to "What do you think? How would you use it?" This encouraged her ingenuity. When children are disregarded, the creative process is stifled.

Avoid providing children with an excessive number of toys, gadgets, electronic games, etc. that do not leave room for creative expression. Instead, provide lots of materials such as colored chalks, paints, different kinds of paper, glitter, glue, styrofoam, cardboard tubes, and materials you might think of as junk. Allow children to experiment, invent their own games, and create new projects. Let them make up their own stories and create the props and background. Encourage them to give presentations of their own: fanciful dramatic masterpieces and dance creations.

Too many parents grumble, "My kids complain that they are bored even though we've bought them everything." Creative kids are not bored. They can find entertainment with two blankets and a picnic table; before long they have a fort and are making up the club rules. Creative kids invent characters for everyone in their games, go on expeditions and rescue the good guys. If parents provide them with a toy for every occasion how can they possibly use their own imaginations? If children spend their time gazing at television, how can they learn to rely on themselves to create fun, challenging, interesting lives?

When children know uniqueness is encouraged and respected, they are more likely to let theirs be discovered. It is your attitude as a parent and how you relate to the special uniqueness of each child that is largely the determining factor. In the words of Wayne Dyer, "Children who are allowed and encouraged to be completely themselves will creatively shine like the noonday sun!"

———■———

8

A Sense of Power

Eleven-year-old Brad got his first job this summer and he's saving up for a mountain bike! Five mornings a week Brad delivers a small local newspaper through the suburbs, and once a month he collects payments from his customers. Brad's mom is raising her children alone and has a minimal amount of time to spend with them, so although she is supportive of Brad's job, the responsibility is totally his. Brad sets the alarm for six a.m., makes his own breakfast, and hikes over to the paper office each morning to begin work. He hasn't missed a day all summer and he figures that by the time school starts in September he'll have that bike, a metallic blue one!

This child believes he can do what he sets out to do in order to reach his goal. He is learning to make his own decisions. He feels competent and confident — competent because his is successful, and confident that he will continue to succeed. This child has what is called "A Sense of Power", which means he feels he can exercise influence on what happens in his life.

Brad's mother is proud of her son. When she observed his stick-to-itiveness on this job, she let him know her support includes partial payment on the bike he wants. This mom believes in encouraging her children to be responsible. She keeps in mind an observation by Booker T. Washington: "Few things help an individual more than to place responsibility on him, and to let him know that you trust him."

BEHAVIOR RELATED TO A SENSE OF POWER

"High P Kids" welcome responsibility and are accustomed to handling it. They are used to being counted

on and have learned to handle the stress that very often is involved. They feel good about taking on new challenges. "Let me give it a try," says a High P Kid. "I think I can handle it." These children are risk-takers, and since in most cases their risking has brought success, they will risk again. They possess big stacks of self-esteem poker chips!

For many Septembers I have watched these children come to school. These are the heads-up kids with open, smiling faces, and "ready for new things" attitudes. Ready to meet new friends, ready to like others and be liked, ready to enjoy the teacher and tackle the schoolwork. These kids just feel good about themselves — they don't know why — they're hung up on feeling good! I once wrote a poem about a High P Kid:

> *I can always do what I set out to do.*
> *Confident, independent; risks are my thing.*
> *I can make decisions problem-solving is fun.*
> *I make my own choices and I'm in charge of me.*

It is important to remember that a sense of power does not mean a wish for control over others. Children like Brad are not manipulative or domineering. They look forward to establishing themselves in a prominent position in the classroom, not by pushing or promoting themselves, but simply by eagerly taking part. High P Kids, confident in the effect they have on their lives, check their options and alternatives and then make their decisions.

Even when children are quite small, parents promote decision-making by offering choices:

> *"Ice cream now or after dinner?"*
> *"Blue jeans or corduroy pants?"*
> *"Clean your room now or just before lunch?"*

Limited choices, as discussed in depth in chapter IV, give children practice making decisions by first looking at alternatives. When parents teach children to make decisions and solve problems, they enhance feelings of independence and personal control.

High P Kids replace the word "problem" with "challenge" and welcome opportunities to excel at what we call problem-solving. This attitude leads to success, in school and out, socially and academically; success produces high self-esteem. Competence breeds confidence; one reinforces the other.

Dave, my younger son, developed a high sense of power as a champion skateboarder for a California team. Workouts were grueling but his perseverance paid off twofold: 1) the winnings he pocketed, and 2) a sense of being in charge of his own life.

This sense of power, the third ingredient in the full-up cup of self-esteem, describes the qualities and behaviors we wish to see in our youth. Imagine a nation of young men and women who, checking their options, choosing between alternatives, and building on competence gained over the years, confidently make their own decisions and accomplish their goals!

CLUES TO A LOW SENSE OF POWER

Once again it is important for parents and teachers to reach the feeling level of children with low self-esteem, in this case a low sense of power. Once again, if we can empathize with the feelings, we can understand why these children resort to defensive, cover-up behaviors. Here is a little poem about a child with a low sense of power:

I am a whiner; it's someone else's fault.
I never get my work done; I'm irresponsible.
Others do things for me so I end up being spoiled.
I get mad a lot, or cry, and I want my own way.

Do you recognize this child and his or her behavior? Children with a low sense of power feel lost. They believe they are victims who are just not lucky, and they convince themselves that they are unable to influence their own lives. Most likely these children live with adults who model this negative attitude. Parents who feel they are victims frequently believe the world is against them. "Things never work out for us," they say. Their children can be heard in school saying, "What's the use of trying?"

With this lack of confidence in themselves, children adopt a variety of cover-up behaviors in order to cope in school.

1) Whining and complaining.

Low P children frequently act helpless and give up easily in the face of frustration. They will use almost any excuse to justify not doing their work. The endless list of aches and pains rarely lacks for originality: "I have this "ouchy" on my fingernail; my appendix hurts; my throat is raspy, and my sleeve is scratching the inside of my arm." In school, these complainers ask for passes to the bathroom or to see the school nurse, or call their moms if they think there's the slightest chance of being rescued.

2) Dawdling and procrastinating.

Very often Low P Kids avoid taking responsibility. Faced with an assignment, they procrastinate, fool around and dawdle. They will promise to do it later, "forget" to do it, or simply leave the scene. At home these same children won't get up on time; they put off getting dressed and doing their work.

By avoiding responsibility, Low P Kids invariably put others into a position of taking it for them. Teachers give them extra help, big sisters baby them and parents end up doing their work. Some of these children become master manipulators, their easiest marks the diligent little girls across the aisle who get inveigled into supplying answers. Sadly enough, every missed opportunity for personal satisfaction causes these children to lose out.

3) Blaming and tattling.

Low P Kids frequently blame others for their problems in life. "My teacher didn't explain the directions," or "Jack made me do it." My favorite is, "He hit me back first!" Perhaps parents of these children do a large amount

---

PUT YOURSELF IN HIS SHOES

Imagine that you are Toby, a nine-year-old student in fourth grade. The trouble is that you just don't dig math. The teacher has been explaining something about divisors and dividends and you are feeling more and more stupid. On your last assignment you got a "D." "It's all Mrs. B's fault," you grumble to yourself. "She didn't teach me to divide. And last year they never taught me my times tables."

When Mrs. B gives the math assignment your tummy begins to hurt and you can't get up the courage to ask for help. So you make the decision to write out all the problems and sneak the answers from your neighbor's paper. "And if she tells on me," you decide, "I'll take this home and get mom to do it."

of blaming also: the boss, the governor, or each other. Their children are in danger of spending a lifetime fearing self-responsibility, and blaming everyone for everything in their lives.

4) Avoiding risks

Some Low P Kids refuse to attempt anything they perceive as challenging, even simple tasks. They never take initiative, but wait for others to take charge and show the way. Because they lack confidence, these kids avoid risks at all costs. To them, risking is so difficult that they quickly learn the axiom: "If I don't risk I can't lose." So they hang back and accept the role of follower, or adopt some other defensive behavior.

Not taking risks is the golden road to avoiding failure. Toby, predicting the grade he will receive — another "D" — cannot risk asking for help or handing in an assignment he has done alone. Because he avoids risking, Toby has not been able to build up his skills in math. Poor skills result in failure, failure lowers his self-esteem, and low self-esteem makes him reluctant to risk meeting the challenges of learning. So his problems are perpetuated. Toby's "golden road" is a vicious circle of failure.

BUILDING A SENSE OF POWER AT SCHOOL

The ideas and techniques described in this section are offered in the hope that parents can gain an understanding of how a sense of power is enhanced in school and can adjust the ideas to the home setting. We all recognize the vital need for self-confidence. It is confidence that allows students to build their own sense of power. As prerequisites, students must:

- possess basic skills
- make choices
- take responsibility

Many students who enter the classroom are well on their way toward meeting these three requirements. Many parents have begun the teaching/guiding process long ago. Frequently however, teachers observe many of the behaviors described in the previous section: whining, complaining, dawdling, procrastinating, blaming, tattling, and avoiding risks. Sometimes teachers wonder where to begin.

CLASSROOM TECHNIQUES

1) Building basic skills

Toby's teacher, Mrs. B., knows to begin by giving him a simple skill diagnosis in math since she knows that a low sense of power is often based on incompetence in some area. Mrs. B. will then make sure Toby is given math assignments at precisely his own ability level. She will hold him responsible for all work assigned, and make sure he does it independently. She may offer a check-list to get him back on track; she definitely will praise his new attempts at independent work and responsibility.

Good teachers know that this combination of academic expectations and personal attention is magical. When skills improve, students begin to realize a sense of power. However, this process takes time, patience and perseverance. Most children who have difficulty learning lack a sense of power, and many must repeat a process again and again. Only when their sense of power begins to rise can they begin to learn effectively.

2) Providing choices

Teachers try to offer many opportunities where choices must be made.

- "Felt pens or colored chalk?"
- "Blue paper or green?"

- "Any kind of report on this book — puppet show? A mural?"

Some teachers hold group discussions that require choice-making. The topics might be:

- "Do you prefer one playmate, or a group?"
- "Is it better to do Monday's homework on Friday or Sunday night?"

Options in class might include:
- A choice of work schedule
- A choice of how an assignment will be done
- A choice of free time activities when work is finished

3) Promoting responsibility

It is obvious to the teacher which of her students have been given small responsibilities since they were very young. Their parents know that children will not become responsible without practice, especially if adults keep doing for them what they can do for themselves. Students reflect this in their actions in school. Teachers foster responsibility in the following ways:

- They divide the classroom maintenance tasks so that each child feels integrally important.
- They give occasional long-term assignments so students can learn to schedule their own time.
- They provide reinforcement for each step completed.
- They help students set concrete, short-term goals that can be achieved in a given length of time.
- They offer students opportunities to improve the classroom climate through class meetings or a suggestion box.
- They teach children to negotiate with others.

HOW PARENTS BUILD A SENSE OF POWER

No component so clearly reflects the environment in which a child is raised as does a sense of power. As a direct result of skillful parenting techniques in a loving home atmosphere, many children exude a confident attitude. They are becoming responsible young citizens in charge of their own lives. The following section describes some of the specific ways this is accomplished in the home.

PUT YOURSELF IN HIS SHOES

You are the daddy of a kindergartener who is still in bed at 8:00 Monday morning. "Where's Joni?" you ask her mother. "Oh, I'm letting her sleep late today. She had a big weekend, you remember, and she went to bed late." Recalling your displeasure with Joni's bedtime behavior, you are doubly unhappy with this announcement. "What about school?" you ask. "Oh, it's only kindergarten. I'll write a note and say she was sick," says mom.

Although you consider yourself a parent-in-training, you do know the value of keeping to a routine. Joni needs a routine to follow for bedtime and all other daily activities. This morning's occurrence causes you no small disappointment. "It's a school day," you say, "and definitely time for Joni to be up and dressed."

1) Develop routines

Parents begin by setting up routines and keeping to them. There are routines for nearly every time slot in the day, from breakfast all the way through to bedtime. For example, on school nights, children are to make their lunches, choose their clothes for the next day, and take a shower. The following demonstrates how a problem can occur in a family with no set routines.

Routines give a feeling of security. Children growing up without them become anxious and confused. Joni, who needs the security of limits, has found she can not only wrangle for a later bedtime and miss school, but that her mother will write a false excuse. Hopefully Joni's daddy will make every effort to establish the needed routines in their home.

PUT YOURSELF IN HIS SHOES

You are Eric, a six-year-old who has been home sick several days with the flu. Your mom cared for you solicitously all through many nights. Now you're fully recovered and back in school, but you still call to her for attention several times a night. One evening your mother announces, "I'm going to sleep all through the night tonight. You'll be fine. If you call me I'm not going to respond."

You are plenty angry, but complaining doesn't work this time.

2) Stick to your decisions

Once routines are established, parents must adhere to them consistently.

Eric's mother is a wise parent. She stated what she would do and remained firm. Eric eventually made his own decision to go to sleep on his own.

Making decisions means not giving in to whining, cajoling, or the misbehavior that I once observed on the sidewalk in front of my house. After they spent a while playing with our cat, my friend was walking home with her daughter, Carrie, who decided she wanted to stay and play. The cat was obliging but mother said no, they were going home now. Carrie whined and begged to stay; mom continued to walk. Carrie threw herself on the grass, screaming; mom walked on without looking back. Glancing up, Carrie jumped to her feet and ran to catch up with her mother. (The cat left the scene.)

This calm, collected mother did not press Carrie with explanations, nor give in to her whining. When Carrie saw that her mother was really going home, she respected the decision. Children can learn limitations only through firm insistence.

3) Use logical consequences.

Consider this mother/daughter exchange:

DeeDee: "Mom, I'm home. Now we can go to the mall."

Mom: "I told you I'd take you shopping if you were home on time. You're an hour late.

DeeDee: "But mother, I have to get new purple earrings!"

Mom: "I'll be driving to the mall again next week. Perhaps you can go with me then."

DeeDee's Mother explained the logical consequences of her tardiness in a kind but firm way . Using logical consequences is an excellent democratic parenting technique and must always be accompanied by a kind, firm attitude. If a child knows that lunchtime is at 12:30 and chooses to play an hour longer, his or her logical consequence is to miss lunch. The logical consequence of dawdling while getting ready for the school bus is walking to school.

Some children will throw a 20-minute tantrum in order to persuade their parents to renege, and some will test parents relentlessly. It is always difficult to remain kind and firm during the testing period. But wise parents will refuse to serve another lunch, or drive the child to school. Firmness always pays off. The length of the tantrums declines, and going without lunch makes a kid mighty hungry. Most important is the long-term result: children who know they have been treated with fairness. Children realize the reasons for cooperating and taking responsibility. This greatly enhances their self-esteem.

4) Promote independence

Debbie is a seven-year-old whose parents are overprotective. Her mother drives Debbie to school each day, walking her to the classroom door and sending her in with admonishments to wear her sweater and be a good girl.

Debbie is a whiner. She dawdles during work time, waiting for the teacher to give her extra attention. She is an expert manipulator who feigns headaches to avoid work and whimpers to be noticed. As a result, Debbie is beginning to fail academically and losing popularity with her peers.

Overprotected children are very frustrating to teachers who see basic intelligence coupled with low achievement. Often it is the parents of these children who come into school saying, "But I know she can do it!" Teachers know it too, and are having to deal with a child who is able to achieve but not doing so.

During conferences, teachers help parents see how they are hindering their children's development, leaving them unable to cope in the world. They explain what's ahead for their children: copying, cheating, giving up, conforming, and later, giving in to "feel-good" remedies like alcohol and drugs, and choosing the wrong people to hang around with. In general, not being in charge of themselves.

Since pampering is so damaging to children, one wonders why parents do it. Perhaps some parents think it is the best way to show love, or perhaps they want to be sure their children don't experience the difficult childhood they had.

Nelsen and Glenn state the problem in their book, *Raising Self-Reliant Children*. "The best way to destroy self-esteem and a sense of self-worth in young people is to do too much for them." [47] I sometimes think that mom finds the library book, zips the jacket and reminds the kid three times to run for the bus. (Then brings him to school when he misses the bus, and drives back home for the library book!)

5) Build self-confidence

One daddy tells about his two-year-old daughter who wanted a drink from the gym water fountain. Busy coaching his son to play basketball, he told her "Sure, honey, go ahead." Minutes later he noticed that the toddler had pushed and dragged a chair to the fountain, climbed up, and was guzzling water.

This dad is promoting confidence and independence. When his son has a little headache he asks if he thinks he can get rid of it without resorting to a pill. He resists the temptation to rush over and check for a skinned knee when his child falls. He avoids giving heavy doses of sympathy which only reinforce whining.

You can foster independence by encouraging a small child to play outside without your presence. Constantly hovering around mom in the house doesn't help little Joey grow up. Encourage older children to take jobs after school, decorate their own rooms, and make their own decisions. Soon they will need to budget their own money, select their own clothes, and choose worthwhile companions. Be supportive of their independence while they go through this in their young lives.

6) Help With Decision-making

Adults create, promote, or allow everything in their lives, and by adulthood, children must do the same: take responsibility for everything that happens to them. From the time they are small, positive everyday interactions with parents and teachers prepare them for this responsibility.

Kids make many, many decisions every day. "How should I answer? Whom should I hang around with? Should I go right home after school? Should I retaliate or ignore the insult? Should I say yes or no? Should I follow my parents' directions or do it my way? Should I conform? Give up? Give in?"

According to Clemes and Bean in *How To Teach Children Responsibility*, "Being able to make decisions well is the chief factor in developing a sense of power or control over one's life. Having such a sense of influence is necessary in order to have high self-esteem and a firm sense of self-worth."[16]

Parents can increase children's ability to make decisions by using three steps:

■ Help the child clarify the problem.

- Help the child check the alternatives.
- Help the child evaluate the consequences of each choice.

Karen didn't have enough money for a gift to take to the party. Her parents helped her see her alternatives: stay home from the party or borrow some money. Karen was helped to evaluate the consequences that included missing the fun and/or having to pay back the loan. Karen had a decision to make; her parents helped with their encouragement.

7) Discourage blaming and tattling

Two favorite behaviors of Low P Kids, we remember, are blaming and tattling. Toby blames his teachers because he hasn't learned his times tables. Most likely, at home he blames siblings, mom, dad and the dog. "The reason kids won't play with me is my little brothers follow me around."

Parents can eliminate the blaming and help Toby find solutions. Perhaps the pre-schoolers need a little of brother's time and attention. Perhaps he could invite a friend to go to a show after he gives his little brothers some of his time and attention.

Tattling can often be eliminated by parents who refuse to listen. An honest statement by an adult to a tattletale is, "I'm not interested in hearing you blame and tattle; you'll have to handle your own problems, and since I know you're a clever child, I'm sure you'll figure something out." Most tattling, I find, is done to get attention or approval from the adult. Children must take responsibility for solving their own problems.

8) Share tasks and responsibilities

The duties and chores required to maintain a home are the responsibility of every family member and should be shared. These jobs are the building blocks that teach responsibility; even the smallest tykes can learn. Danny and David, two-year-old twins, know their jobs — Danny: cars and trucks into the toy box, and David: all toys out of the driveway before daddy comes home. They are proud to have such important jobs, and are learning skills of organization and setting goals while they're still very young.

Some parents find it helpful to set up a Chore Chart that lists all the jobs to be done. All family members — dad, mom, and kids — draw names from a hat and write them next to the jobs in order drawn. Another family has a Job Jar from which they each draw their duties for the week.

Sharing the tasks and chores gives kids a real place in the economy and ecology of the home, and prepares them for the responsibilities to be met at school. Those who have been taught to be responsible at home, to perform duties, and follow parents' guidance, will profit by it throughout their lives.

One of the greatest gifts that adults can give to young people is to help them acknowledge their influence on their own lives. We can do this by giving them many opportunities to make their own decisions and solve their own problems.

9

Together We Make a Difference

We have described constructive and self-destructive behavior in order to discover the feelings that lie hidden underneath. As kid advocates we must continually search for clues to children's self-esteem.

"Together we make a difference" is the unstated premise of this book. I consider the phrase an ideal motto to be adopted by an elementary school, for it signifies a team approach — the collaboration of parents, children, and educators. By working together, we can maximize the innate potential of every child, even those beginning to slip through the cracks.

PUT YOURSELF IN HIS SHOES

Last year in third grade you didn't do so well. But this year your teacher and your parents are collaborating on your education. They have discussed your strengths and special interests, and zeroed in on ways to help you learn better. They even asked your opinion!

As a result you now have a check-list on which you write down your daily assignments and your homework, and check them off as you finish. Your chest swells a little when you think of your new plan and the people who are helping you. It is their love and support that makes you determine to do your very best.

You are a lucky child. The adult in your life are helping you build a future!

Elementary school teachers love to work in communities where parents are interested in their children's education. Parent involvement helps students learn, improves schools, and makes teachers' jobs easier.

HEAVY BURDENS ON OUR SCHOOLS

Many schools are overcrowded, in the midst of financial crunch, dealing with cultural differences or facing racial tension. Class sizes are high; salaries are low. Society foists more and more of its ills upon the schools.

Many of our children live in poverty, and they are particularly vulnerable to health, emotional, social and family problems that can act as barriers to learning. Once in school, disadvantaged students fall farther and farther behind until poor performance, low self-esteem and frustration cause them to drop out.

Today's teachers are responsible for teaching a more sophisticated curriculum to students who are more likely to be below the poverty level, live with only one parent, and come from more varied ethnic backgrounds than at any time in the past. Increasingly, they are asked to teach children who speak a language other than English — in San Diego county, for example, sixty different languages are spoken in the schools. Teachers deal with children who are abused, neglected and homeless. Rather than focusing on just teaching, they very often must cope with kids in the classroom who are not prepared to learn.

In the words of Senator Edward Kennedy, "Teachers often confront directly the grim world of crime, drugs, abuse and neglect that students bring into the classroom. For all that they do, teachers endure unacceptably low salaries and low status."

Some teachers lose hope and leave the profession. Studies show that up to 40 percent of teachers suffer "burnout", become discouraged, and drop out within the first three years. Some drop out without leaving the classroom. Some stay and continue the struggle to create a caring environment in a classroom of 30 students, attempting to meet the needs of the slow learners, the gifted, the misbehavers, and those with untold home problems.

The majority of teachers remain in an increasingly demanding profession believing they can make the world a better place. And they do! Teachers make a tremendous difference in people's lives.

ADVOCATES FOR EDUCATION

Parents should not be strangers to the classrooms in which their children spend so much time, nor to the teachers who share with them the training and motivating of those children. They need to know how the school operates, what problems are facing the school, and how the community can help. They need to examine political platforms carefully and know which candidates can do the most for schools. They need to elect and support school board members who demonstrate a true concern for education.

Parents are in a prime position to help the schools in their constant efforts to overcome the numerous threats to education. By taking part in fiscal and political decision-making at the local level, parents can help establish mutually acceptable goals for schools. This means a commitment of time, energy and good will on the part of everyone. The future of America can only be secured through our children; therefore, our government must be willing to finance education. Armed with the facts, parents can be among the most persuasive supporters of education.

HOMEWORK

Many parents are greatly concerned about homework. "Should I remind my children to do their homework?" parents ask. "How much help should I give? What if the work is done carelessly, or doesn't get done at all? Is it my responsibility? And should I allow the TV to be on, or the stereo to be played?"

Good questions, every one. Children need parents who realize that homework is important and who are concerned about the role that they should play.

Ultimately, it is the child's responsibility to do the homework. But parents have a vital supportive role; their responsibilities lie in these four areas:

1) To decide cooperatively with the child on a time that homework will be done each day, building a consistent, regular routine. When children are included in the decision-making process, they are more likely to cooperate.

2) To set up a working place, preferably a desk or table with a good light — a place of their own — which delivers the message that studying is valued in this home.

3) To be available for brief help when needed, such as going over the directions of an assignment or working through one or two particularly difficult problems. The message to be conveyed is "I care, and I'm here to help if you need it, but I will not do it for you."

4) To bow out. Parents must not deprive the child of taking responsibility because they fear he might fail. Avoid giving more than one reminder. Avoid falling into the trap of a power struggle or a nightly argument. Homework not completed is not the parents' responsibility, and consequences will come from the teacher. The teacher and the student are in the best position to set up logical consequences for not doing work, such as study hall at lunchtime or after school.

Although many children claim they can do homework with the TV on, it is highly likely that they are following the plot of the sit-com more closely than the one in the history book. Insist on absolute quiet during study time, which further reinforces the importance you place on schoolwork.

Helping children to develop good homework habits and to become responsible students is the parents' daily assignment, along with lending constant support. It is wonderful to talk about the assignments after they are completed, but show interest in a conversational tone, not one that checks up on their work. Follow up on a major project by suggesting a family outing to the library, the zoo, a play, or a historical place of interest. Homework can be a jumping-off place for fun and learning for the whole family.

TELEVISION

"Unplug the TV!" demand some child psychologists. They contend that the amount of time spent gazing at the tube is "appalling!" And they cite statistics to support their stand. "The average eight-year-old," they declare, "watches 25 hours of TV a week, 52 weeks a year, which is more than most children spend going to school or in active play."

Neuropsychologists also voice dire warnings. Children in our modern electronic environment are constantly being stimulated from outside so they have little time to reflect and talk to themselves inside their heads. Indeed, one of the most serious charges leveled against TV is that it robs children of the chance to develop their own mental visual imagery that helps in solving math and science problems.

It is no wonder that educators are concerned. Children who are heavy TV watchers, some educators claim, have poorer reading skills, put less effort into school work, and get lower grades. Continuous watching of television programs and commercials reinforces smart-alecky behavior, since virtually all sit-coms use sarcasm, put-downs, and wisecracking as their basis for humor.

But television is here to stay, so I suggest we reach for its positive aspects as much as we can. My suggestions are:

1) Make decisions as a family as to how much TV can be watched on school nights as well as weekends.

2) Determine through careful selection which shows may be viewed.

3) Watch TV with children as often as possible.

Since it is known that violent TV can cause children to become inured to the pain and suffering of others and to behave aggressively, select programs in which characters find nonviolent ways to solve their problems. Constantly guard against glorifying the bad guys who are often promoted by toy manufacturers.

Help your children build critical thinking skills by posing thought-provoking questions about the TV shows you view together. Question the motives of certain characters. Ask, "What would you have done in that situation?" Share your opinions and beliefs and elicit the opinions and beliefs of your children. With a bit of creative thought you can turn TV watching into a valuable learning resource.

It is easy, as we all know, to get flabby and disinterested in life in front of a television set. The less time children spend sitting and being entertained by others, the more time they will have to try new things, create new friends, take charge of their world and be responsible for their own happiness.

BUILDING A LOVE FOR READING

Reading is the basic skill upon which other skills

are built, yet research tells us that the average elementary student spends only seven or eight minutes a day in silent reading at school, and even less at home. In fact, half of all fifth-grade students spend only four minutes a day reading at home as opposed to 130 minutes a day watching TV.

There are many ways you can encourage a love for reading in your children. My magic five tips for parents are:

- Read to them.
- Read with them.
- Read to yourself.
- Listen to them read to you.
- Get hooked on books together.

Read cereal boxes, street signs, menus,magazines, mysteries, travel brochures, gift catalogs, directions for games, jokes, jingles, and jabberwocky. Read whatever your child likes — there is so much to choose from.

Readers are not born, but made! They are made by caring parents and teachers. The amount of reading done *out* of school influences the level of success *in* school.

TIPS FROM TEACHERS

Some of the best people I know are elementary school teachers. They are sensitive, empathetic and intuitive. Some of them seem to possess the ability to understand the problematic idiosyncrasies of kids with whom everybody else has given up. They are indeed special people.

I asked some of those teachers to make a contribution to this chapter. The following are their responses to this question: What do you wish parents would do to help kids succeed in school?

1) Support your children in whatever interest they choose, be it science or music or whatever. Be there if they

need your help, but never take over the project. Thus you will deliver the message that they are capable of succeeding on their own.

2) Let kids be kids. Let them climb trees, get dirty, and while away their afternoons. Let them count ants, play happily in the backyard with the dog. It's good for kids and makes the dog happy! Ease up on too many lessons (karate, piano, diving, ballet, tennis, wrestling, etc.). Ease up on participation in too many clubs, teams, and organized activities.

3) Show your value of education by looking over all papers that come home and attending all school functions. Before a teacher conference, ask the child if there are things he or she would like you to discuss with the teacher.

4) Ask thought-stimulating questions like"What was good about your day?" and "What feelings do you have about this?" Try to avoid questions that require only yes or no answers.

5) Give kids practice using money. Let them help you buy groceries by comparing prices and quantities and estimating the total cost of your order. Let them buy stamps at the post office, and pay for the dry cleaning.

6) Have children keep personal word lists at home. Show them the wonder of a thesaurus. Have a word-of-the-week for the family to share.

7) Show kids you respect them by including their book on the coffee table, and the picture they took in the wall display. Wear the child-made necklace, frame the painting, use the clay jewelry box and let them hear you tell others how much you value it.

8) Let a child write a round-robin letter in a notebook to grandma. Send the notebook back and forth through the

mail. This gives good practice to reluctant writers, (and grandmothers never correct spelling!)

9) Refrain from criticizing a teacher in front of a child.

10) When you come by school, refrain from criticizing the child in his or her presence. Too many parents say "Randy's been such a brat lately. I don't know what's the matter with him." Such a comment is horribly diminishing to a child in front of his teacher.

11) Read to kids, holding them on your lap until they're too big to hold. . .age 12! The message this delivers is: books and love go together.

12) Stay out of the Reminder Business! It's the kids' responsibility to get themselves off to school, and that includes dressing, washing up, watching the clock, eating, and remembering school supplies. An occasional loving reminder is wonderful, but remember: you're there to build responsibility!

13) Don't rescue kids. It robs them of the opportunity to learn by mistakes. Don't put late kids in the car and drive them to school, and don't write an excuse to the teacher!

14) Let the child know he is making a contribution to the family by making the salad, baking the biscuits, mixing the pancakes, etc. This is also an excellent exercise in the skills of measuring, timing, organizing and prioritizing. All are necessary for school success.

15) Encourage hopes and dreams. . .they are fragile and need rich and steady nurturing!

Notes in the Lunchbox

Marta Jean carried a red plastic lunchbox to First Grade with her peanut butter sandwich in it. Sometimes there was a banana and maybe a bag of corn chips. And there was always a note!

Some of the notes in that lunchbox looked like those I've written below. And since Marta Jean still lives in my neighborhood, and now writes notes for her own children's lunchboxes, I know she won't mind that I share them. Perhaps you will borrow a few and add more to the list. My good wishes go with you!

When you get home today, check the cookie jar.
. . .Love, Mommy

Let's play a game of catch after supper.
. . .Love, Dad

It's great for me to watch the new tricks you're learning on the bars. . . .Love, Gram

You're trying hard. . I've been noticing.
. . .Love, Grandpa

*I love you. . .*Love, Mom and Dad

BIBLIOGRAPHY

Borba, Michele and Craig. *Self-Esteem: A Classroom Affair*, vol. 2. San Francisco: Harper & Row, 1982.

Briggs, Dorothy. *Your Child's Self-Esteem*. Garden City, NY: Doubleday, 1970.

Clemes, Harris, and Reynold Bean. *How To Raise Children's Self-Esteem*. Los Angeles: Price/Stern/Sloan, 1987.

Coopersmith, Stanley. *The Antecedents of Self-Esteem*. San Francisco: W.H. Freeman, 1967.

Cutright, Melitta. *The National PTA Talks to Parents. . .How To Get The Best Education For Your Child*. New York: Doubleday, 1989.

Dyer, Wayne. *What Do You Really Want For Your Children?* New York: Wm. Morrow & Co., Inc., 1985.

Glenn, H. Steven and Jane Nelsen. *Raising Self-Reliant Children in a Self-Indulgent World*. Rocklin, CA: Prima Publishing and Communications, 1988.

Hart, Louise. *The Winning Family*. New York: Dodd, Mead & Co., 1987.

Kuczen, Barbara. *Childhood Stress*. New York: Delacorte Press, 1982.

Platt, John. *Life in the Family Zoo*. Sacramento: Dynamic Training and Seminars, 1989.

Purkey, William. *Self-Concept and School Achievement*. Englewood Cliffs, NJ: Prentice-Hall, 1970.

Reasoner, Robert. *Building Self-Esteem*. Palo Alto, CA: Consulting Psychologist Press, Inc., 1982.

Rich, Dorothy, *Mega Skills*. Boston: Houghton Mifflin, 1988.

Smith, Theodore, editor. *Toward A State Of Esteem*. Sacramento: State Dept. of Education, 1990.

Wright, Esther. *Good Morning, Class — I Love You*. Rolling Hills, CA: Jalmar Press, 1989.

Book Order Form

Barbara Reider's books can be purchased through:

Sierra House Publishing
2716 King Richard Drive
El Dorado Hills, CA 95762

Notes in the Lunchbox . . .   9.95
How To Help Your Child
Succeed At School

A Hooray Kind of Kid . . .   8.95
A Child's Self-Esteem
and How to Build It

Please enclose $2.00 for shipping and if you are a
California resident, appropriate sales tax.

Ship to:

Name ———————————————————————————

School/Business ———————————————————————

Street ———————————————————————————

City ——————————— State ——————— Zip ———————